LIGHTHOUSES
Sentinels of the American Coast

Photographs by **Laurence Parent**   *Essay by* **Elinor DeWire**

GRAPHIC ARTS CENTER PUBLISHING®

Text © MMIII by Elinor DeWire
All photographs except archival © MMIII by Laurence Parent
Archival photos courtesy of the owners listed in the photo credits below
Book compilation © MMIII by Graphic Arts Center Publishing®
An imprint of Graphic Arts Center Publishing Company
P.O. Box 10306, Portland, Oregon 97296-0306
503/226-2402
www.gacpc.com

Library of Congress Cataloging-in-Publication data:
Parent, Laurence.
    Lighthouses : sentinels of the American coast / photography by
Laurence Parent ; essay by Elinor DeWire.
        p. cm.
Includes index.
    ISBN 1-55868-698-3 (hardbound)
    1. Lighthouses—United States—Pictorial works. 2.
Lighthouses—United States. I. DeWire, Elinor, 1953- II. Title.
    VK1023.P3 2003
    387.155—dc21
                                                    2002155162

PRESIDENT: Charles M. Hopkins
ASSOCIATE PUBLISHER: Douglas A. Pfeiffer
EDITORIAL STAFF: Timothy W. Frew, Tricia Brown, Jean Andrews, Kathy Howard,
    Jean Bond-Slaughter
PRODUCTION STAFF: Richard L. Owsiany, Joanna M. Goebel
DESIGN: Elizabeth Watson
MAP: Gray Mouse Graphics

ARCHIVAL PHOTO CREDITS: p. 7: National Archives 26-LG-4-5; p. 8: U.S. Coast Guard Archives;
p. 9 (both): U.S. Coast Guard Archives; p. 12 (top): National Archives 26-LG-3-52; p. 13
(top): U.S. Coast Guard Archives; p. 13 (bottom): U.S. Coast Guard Archives; p. 14: Frank
Leslie's Illustrated Newspaper, 1865; p. 15: U.S. Coast Guard Archives; p. 16: U.S. Coast Guard
Archives; p. 21: U.S. Coast Guard Archives; p. 22: National Archives 26-LG-13-20; p. 23:
National Archives 26-LG-69-60; p. 24 (top): National Archives 26-LG-7-11; p. 24 (bottom):
National Archives 26-LG-8-25; p. 27: U.S. Coast Guard Archives; p. 29 (upper left): Nautical
Research Center; p. 29 (lower left): National Archives 26-LG-5-29; p. 29 (lower right):
U.S. Coast Guard Archives; p. 51: Nautical Research Center; p. 52 (both): U.S Coast Guard
Archives; p. 54: U.S Coast Guard Archives; p. 55: U.S Coast Guard Archives; p. 57: National
Park Service, Fort Point National Historic Site; p. 58: National Archives 26-LG-16-52; p. 61:
U.S. Coast Guard Archives; p. 71: National Archives 26-LG-35-1A; p. 72 (left): U.S. Coast
Guard Archives; p. 72 (right): Courtesy of Coastal Georgia Historical Society; p. 73: U.S.
Coast Guard Archives; p. 75 (left): National Archives; p. 75 (right): National Archives,
Second Group 26; p. 77: U.S. Coast Guard Archives; p. 99: U.S. Coast Guard Archives;
p. 107: U.S. Coast Guard Archives.

Printed in the United States of America

▶ RAM ISLAND LEDGE LIGHTHOUSE

Residents of Portland, Maine, lobbied for a lighthouse on hazardous Ram

Island Ledge for more than fifty years before the Lighthouse Board constructed

a seventy-two-foot granite tower for the sea-washed site in 1905. It guides

shipping into Maine's busiest harbor.

▲ TAWAS POINT LIGHTHOUSE, WESTERN SHORE, LAKE HURON

LIGHTHOUSES OF THE AMERICAN COAST

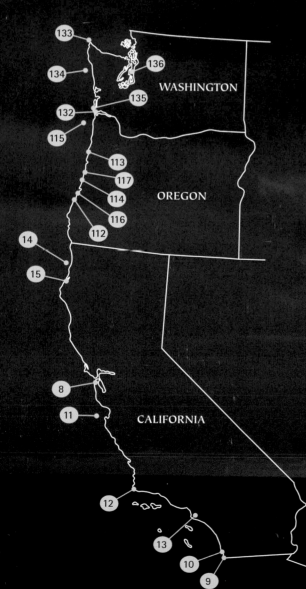

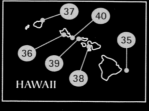

ALABAMA
1 Sand Island

ALASKA
2 Cape Decision
3 Cape Hinchinbrook
4 Cape Sarichef
5 Eldred Rock
6 Scotch Cap
7 Sentinel Island

CALIFORNIA
8 Mile Rocks
9 New Point Loma
10 Old Point Loma
11 Pigeon Point
12 Point Conception
13 Point Vicente
14 St. George Reef
15 Trinidad Memorial

CONNECTICUT
16 Five Mile Point
17 Lynde Point
18 New London Harbor

DELAWARE
19 Delaware Breakwater East
20 Fenwick Island
21 Harbor of Refuge

FLORIDA
22 Cape Canaveral
23 Cape Florida
24 Cape San Blas
25 Cape St. George
26 Carysfort Reef
27 Egmont Key
28 Key West
29 Pensacola
30 Sanibel Island
31 St. Augustine
32 St. Marks

GEORGIA
33 St. Simon's Island
34 Tybee Island

HAWAII
35 Cape Kumukahi
36 Diamond Head
37 Kilauea Point
38 Lahaina Harbor
39 Lauu Point
40 Makapu'u Point

INDIANA
41 Michigan City

LOUISIANA
42 Chandeleur Island
43 New Canal
44 Sabine Pass
45 Southwest Reef
46 Tchefuncte River

MAINE
47 Bass Harbor Head
48 Cape Elizabeth
49 Cape Neddick
50 Doubling Point Range Lights
51 Fort Point Range Lights
52 Marshall Point
53 Matinicus Rock
54 Monhegan Island
55 Owls Head
56 Pemaquid Point
57 Portland Head
58 Ram Island Ledge
59 Rockland Breakwater
60 West Quoddy Head

MARYLAND
61 Concord Point
62 Thomas Point

MASSACHUSETTS
63 Boston Harbor
64 Highland
65 Marblehead Neck
66 Scituate

MICHIGAN
67 Au Sable Point
68 Big Sable
69 Eagle Harbor
70 Fort Gratiot
71 Lightship *Huron*
72 Little Sable Point
73 Ludington North Pierhead
74 Manistee North Pierhead
75 Marquette Harbor
76 Old Mackinac
77 Old Presque Isle
78 Point Betsie

79 Point Iroquois
80 Pointe Aux Barques
81 Port Sanilac
82 Presque Isle
83 Seul Choix
84 South Haven
85 St. Joseph North Pier
86 Sturgeon Point
87 Tawas Point

MINNESOTA
88 Grand Marais Front Range
89 Split Rock

MISSISSIPPI
90 Biloxi

NEW HAMPSHIRE
91 Portsmouth Harbor

NEW JERSEY
92 Barnegat
93 Cape May
94 Hereford Inlet
95 Navesink Twin Lights
96 Sandy Hook
97 Sea Girt

NEW YORK
98 Buffalo Main
99 Fire Island
100 Fort Niagara
101 Hudson-Athens
102 Montauk Point
103 Saugerties
104 Tibbetts Point

NORTH CAROLINA
105 Bald Head
106 Bodie Island
107 Cape Hatteras
108 Cape Lookout
109 Currituck Beach
110 Ocracoke

OHIO
111 Marblehead

OREGON
112 Cape Arago
113 Cape Meares

CAPE MAY LIGHTHOUSE, NEW JERSEY

THE 1902 ROCKLAND BREAKWATER LIGHTHOUSE ON THE TIP OF A 0.9-MILE-LONG BREAKWATER, ROCKLAND HARBOR, MAINE

Introduction

The night is dark, and I am far from home . . .

—Cardinal John Henry Newman

A few hours before midnight on October 10, 1492, Christopher Columbus stood alone on the forecastle of the flagship *Santa Maria*. Throughout the day, signs of land had appeared in the water—a reed, a cane pole, a sandpiper—and extra lookouts had been posted on all three ships. As Columbus peered into the darkness, his men slept fitfully in their straw beds, dreaming of rich lands, pure water, sumptuous feasts, and gold. Their leader dreamed too. As a young boy he had journeyed to the lighthouse at Genoa, Italy, where his uncle was the lightkeeper. He had climbed the tower at dusk and seen the great fire beacon kindled, its golden light spilling over the harbor in welcome rays. He had looked out to sea, incredulous that ships grew smaller and disappeared. Always, he had yearned to travel beyond the distant horizon.

The admiral was the first to see the glimmer of light on the sea horizon, "like a wax candle rising and falling," he said. It was so faint. He doubted his eyes and fetched another man to look and he, too, saw the feeble light. A bonfire, perhaps? Columbus gathered his lookouts and prayers were offered. He admonished them to keep good watches, for the first man to sight land would be rewarded handsomely with money and a silk doublet.

The next day, more signs floated in the sea. More prayers were said and more lookouts posted. The caravel *Pinta* took the lead, as she had the best pilot and was the most maneuverable. Columbus steered a course west toward the light he had seen the night before. Two hours after midnight on Friday, October 12,

▲ St. Augustine Lighthouse, Florida

Mount Desert Rock Lighthouse, Maine

1492, with a bright moon illuminating the sea, the lookout in the crow's nest of the *Pinta* cried out, "Land! Land!"

That Columbus's welcome to the New World came in the form of a light, a bonfire burning on a distant shore, should be no surprise. Bonfires were the customary beacons for navigation before formal lighthouses were built. The natives of San Salvador,

where Columbus made landfall, were sailors too, their lives regulated by ocean highways connecting the many islands of the Caribbean. It's doubtful that they sensed at the time how significant their crude fire beacon would be for the weary seamen of the three tiny ships—and for the course of modern history.

LIGHTING THE COLONIES

More than two centuries would pass before a formal lighthouse in America replaced crude bonfires. Colonists made their way to the Chesapeake Bay and into the James River in 1607 without the benefit of a single navigational aid, and weary Pilgrims arrived in Plymouth Harbor in 1620 lacking any beacons whatsoever. Survival was the primary concern for a time, but the colonies soon began to petition England for funds to build lighthouses. Parliament was slow to respond, despite the British Admiralty's insistence that good navigational lights were desperately needed in the colonies, and would benefit the Mother Country through safer access for her own vessels and increased commerce with other nations.

Pole beacons of burning pitch were set up at places like Point Allerton on the approach to Boston; Sandy Hook, south of New York Harbor; Cape Henlopen, at the mouth of the Delaware Bay; and Tybee Island, at the entrance to the Savannah River. There was a rumor that the French had a light at the mouth of the Mississippi River and the Spanish had a beacon of sorts in the watchtower at St. Augustine. Under pressure from the Massachusetts Bay Colony, and determined not to have its American settlements labeled uncivilized by the rest of Europe, Parliament approved a lighthouse for Boston Harbor in 1713—but colonists had to fund the project on their own. The colonists decided to levy a duty of a penny per ton on all large ships entering and leaving Boston Harbor, and use the proceeds to build and maintain the lighthouse.

Lighthouses soon were raised at other sites, including the busy ports of Nantucket and New London, the entrance to

◄ *An artist's rendering of the 1847 Mount Desert Rock Lighthouse, twenty-six miles from shore in the Gulf of Maine.*

► *The Cape Henlopen Lighthouse, the seventh lighthouse erected in the American Colonies, was built on unstable sand dunes in 1767 and waged a 147-year battle with erosion before its collapse in April 1926.*

CAPE HENLOPEN LIGHTHOUSE, DELAWARE BAY, THE DAY BEFORE ITS COLLAPSE

THE FIRST LIGHTHOUSE

Long after the great Pharos Lighthouse fell into the harbor at Alexandria, Egypt, artists attempted to re-create its image from ancient descriptions. Believed to be the tallest lighthouse in recorded history, at over 450-feet, it stood nearly fifteen centuries before erosion and repeated earthquakes toppled it.

On the bottom of the Nile Estuary, partially obscured by silt, lies the wreckage of a once-majestic edifice. Sprigs of coral festoon the marble faces of its ancient gods, and seaweed curtains undulate over its shattered marble and granite blocks, veiling the past in mystery. The ruins—an estimated fifty million cubic feet of stone—easily cover several acres of seafloor and are visible from the air.

This rubble is all that remains of the great Pharos of Alexandria, the earliest known lighthouse. Built about 279 B.C. at the mouth of the Nile River, it towered more than 450 feet over the harbor and was the tallest structure of its day. The lantern held a massive stone furnace that consumed forests of wood from inland Africa and tested the resolve of its keepers, who toiled in a continuous procession hauling fuel up and ashes down. By day, a curl of smoke guided ships from afar; by night, the great fire

PHAROS LIGHTHOUSE, ALEXANDRIA, EGYPT

beacon shone miles out to sea, its light amplified by a large mirror.

Pharos (whose Greek name means "beacon") stood for more than fifteen hundred years, the longest tenure of any lighthouse in recorded history. It remained lit until the tenth century, when the island on which it stood was ransacked by Byzantine treasure hunters who dismantled the beacon, stole the great mirror, and destroyed the lantern. Erosion gnawed at the island until the fourteenth century, when an earthquake and subsequent tidal wave toppled the lighthouse into the harbor. Divers located its remains in the 1980s, and the city of Alexandria, Egypt, is currently at work on a full-size replica of the lighthouse.

PHAROS LIGHTHOUSE, ALEXANDRIA, EGYPT

The oldest standing light tower in the nation, the Sandy Hook Lighthouse has served shipping headed into New York Harbor since 1764.

the Narragansett and Delaware bays, Charleston Harbor, and the Savannah River. By the start of the American Revolution, eleven lighthouses shone over colonial waters. Nine stood in the Northeast, the hub of American maritime activity, where large

ports thrived as trading and whaling centers. Most were damaged or entirely destroyed in the war, but rebuilding began soon after independence was gained. On August 7, 1789, the fledgling federal government assumed control of all lighthouses and placed them in the care of the Treasury Department under Alexander Hamilton. Realizing that lighthouses represented civility in world commerce, and were an obvious boon to merchants and shipmasters, Hamilton urged President George Washington to close the dark gaps along the busy American coast.

THE LIGHT HOUSE ESTABLISHMENT

An organization within the Treasury Department known simply as the "Light House Establishment" was created and quickly went to work. The first hazardous shore to be marked was the entrance to the Chesapeake Bay at Cape Henry. Completed in 1791, this was soon followed by lights on Bald Head at the mouth of the Cape Fear River; Portland Harbor and Kennebec River in Maine; Montauk Point and Eatons Neck on Long Island; and Salem Harbor, Newburyport, Martha's Vineyard, and the dangerous backside beach of Cape Cod in Massachusetts. By 1800, there were twenty-three lighthouses in the United States, yet only six were located south of Connecticut, since New England still dominated maritime activity. They were now the responsibility of the Commissioner of Revenue, an office Alexander Hamilton created in part to address the rise in commerce lighthouses had produced.

Another twenty-six lighthouses were in service by 1820. During this period the Light House Establishment changed administration several times and ultimately landed in the hands of the Fifth Auditor of the Treasury, Stephan Pleasanton, the nation's fiscal manager. Lighthouses had become a burden on the national budget by this time, and Pleasanton clutched the purse strings tightly. His penchant for accepting the lowest bid and his lack of knowledge about lighthouse construction and illumination hampered his work. He relied on the advice of a self-serving contractor named Winslow Lewis of Wellfleet,

SANDY HOOK LIGHTHOUSE, NEW JERSEY

Massachusetts, and awarded him most of the bids. He also allowed local collectors of customs in various ports to oversee construction contracts. Before long, political favoritism and fraud arose. Though 270 lighthouses were built during Pleasanton's tenure from 1820 to 1851—covering the entire Eastern Seaboard, the eastern Gulf of Mexico, and extending into the Great Lakes— many were of poor quality and inferior to the lights in Europe.

Pleasanton did, however, introduce several important technologies. Range lights, or leading lights, were established in channels to keep vessels on course as they went into port. The first set of range lights marked the winding Savannah River Channel in 1820. Also that year, lightships were commissioned to allow lights to show offshore where lighthouse towers could not yet be built. The problem of fog was addressed during this period as well. Cannons had been used at Boston Light and Beavertail Point Light to assist the mariner when a beacon was obscured in poor visibility, but firing them every half hour proved expensive and they were easily confused with ships' cannons. The clarion tones of church bells seemed to carry well over water, so Pleasanton ordered a fogbell cast in 1820 for murky West Quoddy Head Lighthouse at the entrance to the Bay of Fundy. Its success led to the adoption of fogbells for lighthouses throughout the nation.

Straight pile and screwpile lighthouses were introduced in the 1840s toward the end of Pleasanton's administration. Though uncomely, they could be anchored securely with piles driven deep into the unstable beds of bays, rivers, and backwaters, thus allowing lighthouses to be positioned offshore. Straight piles worked in moderately wet, alluvial seabeds, while screwpiles were anchored where a layer of silt and muck existed. These designs were ideal in the Chesapeake region and Carolina sounds. Most were quaint, little wooden houses perched on iron pile or screwpile foundations, but later designs for the Florida Reef and Gulf of Mexico evolved into monstrous hulks of metal from top to bottom, towering more than a hundred feet over the open sea.

DOUBLING POINT RANGE LIGHTS, KENNEBEC RIVER, MAINE, THE ONLY ACTIVE RANGE LIGHTS IN MAINE

Pleasanton also inaugurated the tradition of lighthouse tenders, special vessels assigned to build, repair, and provision lighthouses, as well as transport personnel. They became the lifeline for lightkeepers sequestered on remote islands and waterbound towers. Families cheered the sound of tender whistles, a signal that meant the arrival of mail, visitors, perhaps a doctor to look after a sick child, or a minister to perform a baptism or wedding. Even a milk cow or a piano might be delivered, sometimes lifted onto a light station by a derrick and boom.

Despite many changes and improvements, mariners worldwide criticized American lighthouses, calling them mediocre at best. A major complaint concerned the outdated illuminating equipment in use. Argand lamps intensified by silvered parabolic reflectors had been upstaged by prismatic Fresnel lenses in the 1820s, which increased brilliance; yet the United States had failed to adopt the technology, largely due to Pleasanton's excessive penny-pinching. In response to complaints, Congress divided the coast into six districts in 1838 and assigned military officers to survey each district and submit reports on the condition and operation of lighthouses. Their findings were consistent. Lightkeepers were not adequately trained, paid, or supervised, and many lights were in disrepair. Lanterns were not properly fitted, causing leaks and deterioration of wood, stone, and metal. Contract specifications had been shortcut or ignored at a number of lighthouses to save money, and knowledgeable engineers had not supervised the work. Worst, the lights themselves were outdated, some so short and poorly illuminated as to render more confusion for the mariner than assistance.

Two prism lenses were ordered from Paris for a hefty price tag of $24,000, and installed for testing in the Navesink Twin Lights in New Jersey in 1841. The new beacons quickly proved far superior to the antiquated reflector system then in use throughout the United States. Additional investigations confirmed the need for change and convinced Congress that a complete overhaul of the Light House Establishment was needed. It would

THE TWIN LIGHTS AT MATINICUS ROCK, CIRCA 1890S, WERE MANNED BY THREE KEEPERS AND THEIR FAMILIES.

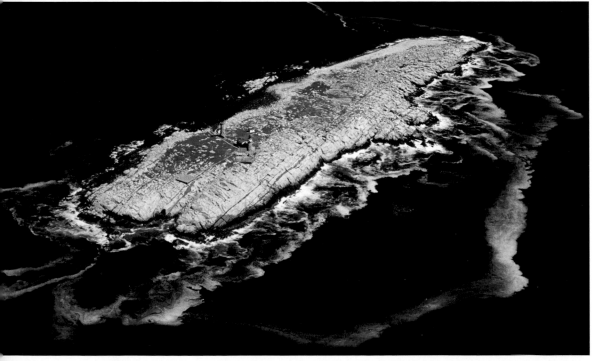

MATINICUS ROCK, A BOULDER STREWN ISLAND TWENTY-THREE MILES OFF THE MAINE COAST

take a decade for the new regime to be put in place, and Pleasanton would endure repeated censure. Yet, upon his dismissal in 1851, 335 lighthouses and lightships and 50 fog signals were on duty in the United States.

THE ERA OF THE LIGHTHOUSE BOARD

In 1852, the nine-member Lighthouse Board was created, composed of representatives from the navy and army, the Corps of Topographical Engineers, the Coast Survey, and civilian scientists. The board reorganized districts and appointed inspectors and engineers to run them. Collectors of customs were retained for administrative purposes but greatly downgraded in decision-making authority. Lighthouses were rebuilt and updated with modern construction materials and lighting technologies, and new stations were added to light dark shores. Additional tenders went into service, and depots were established within districts to facilitate management of the many navigational aids, which now included more than two thousand lights, buoys, daymarks, and fog signals.

Lightkeepers were selected with greater care and given apprentice-type training, uniforms, and rank. Regular inspections were conducted and merit awards were given for exceptional performance. The emphasis on a better life for lighthouse families meant improving living quarters, sending teachers to remote sites to educate the children, providing portable libraries to be exchanged between stations, and scheduling more frequent visits from the supply ships.

A period of massive renewal had begun, stifled only by the Civil War a decade later. The South launched its own Confederate States Lighthouse Bureau but soon abandoned the effort when the military officers overseeing it were called into battle. Lightkeepers in the South were forced to choose sides. Many deserted their stations under duress from Rebel sympathizers or when raiding parties arrived. Towers were burned or battered by cannon fire, their costly prism lenses were destroyed or

MAINE'S MOUNT DESERT ROCK LIGHTHOUSE IN THE 1880S, WITH FOGBELL

THE SIDEWHEELER TENDER *HOLLY*, CIRCA 1910, AT POINT NO POINT LIGHTHOUSE, CHESAPEAKE BAY

disassembled and buried, and oil was dumped in the sand. When the conflict ended, a fifth of the nation's lighthouses needed urgent repair and reinstatement.

As Reconstruction began, the Lighthouse Board committed itself to better methods of construction, illumination, and sound signaling. Engineers were sent abroad to study various kinds of lighting apparatuses and fuels, as well as architectural styles.

◄ *Lighthouse tenders, sturdy vessels that built, maintained, and provisioned lighthouses, were the keepers' lifeline to shore. Larger tenders, like* Holly, *were named for trees. Smaller tenders wore floral names.*

► *Many Southern lighthouses were damaged or destroyed during the Civil War. Mobile Point Lighthouse's illuminating apparatus was removed and hidden by Confederates in 1861, and the building was irreparably damaged by Union gunners in 1864.*

►► *Cast iron became the material of choice for lighthouses in the mid-nineteenth century. Iron towers were cheap to produce, quick to assemble, sturdy, and moveable. The spiral stairway and walls of Matagorda Island Lighthouse were fabricated in a Baltimore foundry and transported to Texas by ship.*

MOBILE POINT LIGHTHOUSE, ALABAMA, 1864 CIVIL WAR DAMAGE

The second half of the nineteenth century became an era of monumental building and improved illumination. Iron replaced wood and stone as a cheaper and more durable material for tower walls, lanterns, and stairways. Pile-design and caisson lighthouses of various types rose in places where wind and water would quickly damage a masonry tower or an unstable foundation existed. Great wave-swept lighthouses were built on hazardous offshore sites by a new fleet of highly specialized tenders. Despite their rowdy crews and tough duty, the Lighthouse Board named these vessels after flowers, shrubs, and trees native to the regions where they worked. *Maple, Sassafras,* and *Mistletoe* worked northeast waters; *Arbutus* and *Geranium* served the South and Gulf of Mexico. The Great Lakes were tended by *Amaranth* and *Walnut. Madrono* and *Fir* plied the West Coast and Alaska, and *Kukui* served Hawaii.

New fuels and optics were tested in a special experimental lighthouse at the Staten Island Lighthouse Depot and at nearby Navesink Twin Lights in New Jersey. Kerosene, which burned cleaner, cheaper, and more efficiently than whale oil, was adopted for use in 1878. Incandescent oil vapor lamps went into use in the 1880s and acetylene gas lamps a decade later. Electricity made its debut in 1886 in the Statue of Liberty—an official lighthouse until 1902—and began appearing in other lighthouses around 1900. Better sound signals were developed and tested at Beavertail Lighthouse in Rhode Island, one of the foggiest stations in the nation. Automatic strikers were devised for fogbells, and in some places the bells were replaced by louder steam-powered trumpets, whistles, sirens, and horns. An age of mechanization had firmly taken hold.

By this time, Congress was considering disbanding the Lighthouse Board and moving its operations to the Commerce Department, where they would again be under civilian control. Although the board had worked miracles, it was deemed too militaristic and hardhanded, and lighthouses more logically fell under the aegis of commerce than defense. In 1910 the reign of the Lighthouse Board officially ended and the Bureau of Lighthouses was created. Its superintendent was a capable and zealous public servant from the U.S. Coast and Geodetic Survey named George Putnam. He inherited 9,804 navigational aids, 1,462 of them lighthouses. Over the next twenty-five years he streamlined the service and moved it into an era of modernization and automation.

THE LIGHTHOUSE TENDER *HIBISCUS* SERVED SOUTHERN WATERS FROM 1908 TO 1946.

CAST-IRON STAIRS, MATAGORDA ISLAND LIGHTHOUSE, TEXAS

THE MODERN ERA

A priority for Putnam was personnel. Some fifteen thousand employees worked in the bureau at this time, and two new districts recently had been added in Alaska and Hawaii. Putnam launched an in-house newsletter to educate and recognize his staff, and campaigned tirelessly on their behalf through public appearances and interviews that extolled the work of lighthouse keepers. In 1918 he procured a long-awaited pension plan, enabling personnel over age seventy-five to retire.

Modernizing the service was an equally important focus. Putnam made a thorough inventory of all aids to navigation and carefully determined where he could reduce costs. He discontinued multiple lights, which had long been unnecessary due to flash characteristics introduced in the nineteenth century. He

▲ *In 1869, the U.S. Lighthouse Board began a tradition of naming its work ships, called tenders, after flowers, shrubs, and trees native to the regions where they served. The* Hibiscus *worked in southern waters following the Civil War. A service flag featuring a small blue lighthouse flew from her mainmast.*

ELDRED ROCK LIGHTHOUSE, LYNN CANAL, ALASKA

and moved lighthouses into the care of the U.S. Coast Guard, an organization less than twenty-five years old. Many lighthouse personnel objected, citing the Coast Guard as more suited to policing the sea and saving lives than operating navigational aids. As propitiation, lightkeepers were invited to enter the ranks at levels commensurate with experience or retain their civilian status until retirement.

As would be expected, the character of the personnel and of the lighthouses themselves changed tremendously in the decades that followed. Technology was the primary agent of change. By the end of World War II all lights were electrified, and many were converted to automatic operation, enabling the Coast Guard to remove resident keepers and assign them to other jobs. The cost savings was enormous, especially at remote and waterbound lighthouses where access was difficult and crews suffered loneliness and occasional deprivation.

A massive automation program initiated in the 1960s finished the work George Putnam had begun half a century before. Durable plastic optics requiring little care replaced classic glass lenses. Automatic light and fog sensors upstaged lightkeepers. Lightbulb changers rotated new bulbs into position when old ones burned out, backup generators sat ready in case of sudden loss of power, and solar panels economically supplanted domestic power lines as a dependable source of energy. Robot lighthouses were connected to a computerized alarm system that alerted the Coast Guard if a light went out or a fog signal failed. By 1995 only one lighthouse in the nation continued to operate with resident lightkeepers: Boston Light retained its Coast Guard crew as figureheads—symbolic keepers to commemorate a long and faithful chapter in American history.

As lighthouses segued into the modern era, new problems arose, namely vandalism and neglect. Grounds lost their groomed appearance, since they were visited only a few times a year by maintenance crews. Defacement and theft was widespread, necessitating sealed windows and heavy locks on all buildings.

Marking the far-flung shores of Alaska tested the mettle of lighthouse builders and lighthouse keepers. In 1908, the lonely guardian of Eldred Rock stood a difficult vigil on this sequestered point of perpetual rain and fog along Lynn Canal in the Inside Passage. The octagonal Eldred Rock Lighthouse still stands and is the oldest original sentinel in Alaska.

introduced radio communications, and sturdier new building materials such as reinforced concrete and steel. More importantly, he emphasized the development and testing of automatic devices that would supercede human hands in keeping the lights and fog signals. By the time Putnam retired in 1935, many old, unneeded sentinels had been removed from service and the active fleet was well on its way to self-sufficiency.

Putnam's successor, Harold King, continued the modernization agenda, but he had barely settled into the superintendent's chair when President Franklin Roosevelt reorganized the service again

BOSTON LIGHTHOUSE, MASSACHUSETTS

◄ *Yankee simplicity and sturdiness is the signature of Boston Lighthouse. The tower dates back to 1783 when it was rebuilt, possibly from granite blocks from the original 1716 lighthouse, destroyed by the British during the American Revolution. Anchor bands support the old masonry and a fresh coat of white paint provides a bright daymark.*

► *Monhegan Island Lighthouse, ten miles off the mid-Maine coast, is among many that have been saved by the Historic Lighthouse Preservation Act of 2002. Both an active navigational aid and a museum, the lighthouse houses Monhegan Historical and Cultural Museum in the keeper's quarters.*

Even so, graffiti continued, and many towers became eyesores. The Coast Guard lacked the funds and manpower for the upkeep of lighthouses, but recognized their historic value.

Preserving the historic integrity of old lighthouses while they continued in service, minus resident keepers, became a critical issue in the 1980s. Many decommissioned lights found new life as museums and centerpieces in parks, cared for by state and private groups or by the National Park Service. For active, automated lighthouses, especially those at remote locations, the story played out differently. With its budget strained in the late 1990s, the Coast Guard announced that it could no longer maintain the old structures. Congress rallied, and the Historic Lighthouse Preservation Act was passed in 2002, providing for the transfer of all existing lighthouses, active or decommissioned, into public hands and setting forth guidelines for their stewardship.

The legislation assured that these aging, cherished landmarks will be preserved for future generations. At the same time, it also created a new age of keepership. Small community groups, such as historical societies, yacht clubs, and Scout troops, as well as museums and large institutions like the American Lighthouse Foundation and the U.S. Lighthouse Society, may adopt lighthouses and maintain them for educational use. The many individuals and groups who care for and interpret old lighthouses are a new breed of lightkeepers. In some sense, their work retains the character of the traditional "wickies" of long ago: they maintain the grounds and buildings, and keep the light clean and bright and the fog signal working. They raise the flag every day and greet visitors, record the weather, and write in the daily journal. What's different is the purpose of their work.

Lightkeepers are no longer required; their vigil is voluntary. They keep the lighthouses out of reverence for an occupation now obsolete.

Sighing, I climbed the lighthouse stair . . .
And while the day died, sweet and fair,
   I lit the lamps again.

                        Celia Thaxter
                    The Wreck of the Pocahontas

MONHEGAN ISLAND LIGHTHOUSE, TEN MILES OFF THE MAINE COAST

HEREFORD INLET LIGHTHOUSE

FORT NIAGARA LIGHTHOUSE

SEA GIRT LIGHTHOUSE

NAVESINK TWIN LIGHTS, BUILT IN 1872, NEW JERSEY HIGHLANDS

◄ ◄ *(Top row) The Carpenter Gothic Style Hereford Inlet Lighthouse, North Wildwood, New Jersey, built 1874.*
◄ *Fort Niagara Lighthouse built in 1818, the first lighthouse in the Great Lakes.*
◄ ◄ *(Bottom row) Sea Girt Lighthouse, built in 1896, between Navesink and Barnegat, New Jersey.*
◄ *Resembling a Bastille fortress, Navesink Twin Lights' north tower is connected to its sibling by the old keepers' quarters. Built in 1872 to replace an earlier set of twin lights, the brownstone towers stand on the New Jersey Highlands, 254 feet above sea level. For many years, they were a testing station for illuminants used in American lighthouses.*

THE 1835 PEMAQUID POINT LIGHTHOUSE, ONE OF MAINE'S PRETTIEST, WEST SIDE OF MUSCONGUS BAY

Lighthouses of the Northeast

MAINE TO MARYLAND

The story of America's lighthouses began in New England and the Mid-Atlantic states. Here, the first settlements sprang up, accessible only by ship and obstructed by perilous rocks, reefs, and sandbars. A jagged coastline, punishing nor'easters, and bouts of thick fog challenged vessels seeking a safe harbor, and underscored the need for lighthouses. But lack of money and a disinterested Mother Country hindered all efforts until 1716, when the first American lighthouse was established at the entrance to Boston Harbor.

The forty-foot tower was built of granite rubblestone on Little Brewster Island. A small house stood next to it for the keeper and his family, and there was grass for chickens and a cow. George Worthylake lit the lantern's forty-six-candle chandelier for the first time on the night of September 16, 1716, expecting to earn a meager salary of £50 per year. A few months later, he drowned while returning to the island in his boat; also lost were his wife and daughter, and a black slave. Tragedy seemed to mark the lighthouse. Its second keeper also drowned, and lightning repeatedly struck it. Though the Puritans felt that the newly invented lightning rod was an affront to heaven's divine power, they made an exception for Boston Light after lightning set it on fire in 1751.

The light's early years were difficult, but the worst was yet to come. During the American Revolution, British troops occupied the lighthouse and used it as a lookout for spying on activities in the harbor. In 1775, Patriots stormed the island and set fire to the lighthouse, rendering it useless. The following year, the tower was blown up by the British as they retreated from the harbor,

▲ HIGHLAND LIGHTHOUSE
Cape Cod's Highland Lighthouse was established in 1797.

BOSTON LIGHTHOUSE

21

and it collapsed. By this time, ten other light towers stood in the colonies, and most were damaged or destroyed during the war as well. Sandy Hook Lighthouse at the entrance to New York Bay was scarred by cannonballs. Cape Henlopen Light on the southern shores of Delaware Bay was guarded by American militia for a time, then gutted by fire.

Seven lighthouses in the Northeast that were not seriously damaged survived the conflict and were soon back in service. Most were situated at important whaling and fishing ports, such as Nantucket, New London, Salem, and Portsmouth. Beavertail Light guarded the treacherous Narragansett Bay leading into Providence, and a tiny set of wooden twin lights shone from a

sandspit off Plymouth. Boston Light was quickly rebuilt and returned to service in 1783. Six years later, the new federal government assumed control of lighthouses and began the expensive task of building new ones.

By 1800, twenty-two lighthouses were on duty from Maine to Maryland. Of critical importance was Montauk Point Light at the tip of Long Island—the welcome beacon for ships arriving from Europe. Its construction was ordered by President George Washington as one of his first official duties. He took special care in approving its location, cautioning the builder that erosion on the point was a concern and that the tower needed to be situated three hundred feet back from the cliff. The sturdy design—a

◄ *A painting of the first Boston Lighthouse, built in 1716, was commissioned by the Coast Guard in honor of the light's 275th anniversary. The tower was scarred by fire, lightning, and human tragedy before its ultimate demise in 1776 when retreating British troops destroyed it.*

► *A sturdy octagonal stone design was adopted for nearly all early American lighthouses. The sentinels at Montauk Point, Long Island, and New London Harbor, Connecticut, built in 1797 and 1800, were nearly identical. New London Harbor Light is pictured with its 1880s keeper. Montauk Point Light, two feet shorter than its Connecticut compatriot, currently wears a brown band as a daymark. Though aging, both lighthouses remain active and architecturally sound.*

MONTAUK POINT LIGHTHOUSE, LONG ISLAND, NEW YORK

NEW LONDON HARBOR LIGHTHOUSE, CONNECTICUT

THE LADY LIGHTKEEPER OF LIME ROCK

Ida Lewis is one of many women who served at American lighthouses, taking up the duties after the death of a father, husband, or brother.

IDA LEWIS, THE INTREPID LADY LIGHTKEEPER OF LIME ROCK LIGHTHOUSE

The history of lightkeeping is rife with heroes who stood by their beacons through all manner of travail, and performed incredible feats of bravery. A romance of sorts surrounds their duty, and beguiles us with a reassuring stereotype—the lightkeeper as a wise, white-whiskered old man hobbling about on sea legs, ever vigilant for a ship in distress.

Most were men, but into this largely male occupation a few women dared to step. They were usually wives, daughters, or sisters of the keepers, and obtained their jobs after apprentice-type training. Many were "lighthouse widows," promoted after the death of their husbands.

Such was the case of Ida Lewis. Her father was appointed to tiny Lime Rock Lighthouse in Newport, Rhode Island, in 1853 (when Ida was only eleven years old), but poor health encumbered his work. He later came to depend greatly on his daughter who, it's said, was the true keeper of the light. She could handle a boat as well as a man and knew the vagaries of the harbor. Night after night, assisting her father, she learned to tend the beacon and assumed full care of it after a stroke left him disabled.

A cold March 1869 rescue of two men drowning in Newport Harbor earned the twenty-seven-year-old an interview with *Harper's Weekly* and a full-length portrait on its July cover. President Ulysses S. Grant came to visit her at the lighthouse, and the city held a festival in her honor. Other rescues followed, and by 1872, when her father died, Ida Lewis was world famous. People affectionately called her "America's Grace Darling," after a young English girl who had gained fame as a rescuer at Longstone Lighthouse in 1838.

Ida thought she was assured the job of lightkeeper after her father's death, but the government hedged. She was considered too young for such a grave responsibility, so her mother was appointed instead. There were protests, but not from Ida. She quietly assisted at the lighthouse until her mother announced her retirement in 1879, and then Ida reapplied for the job. This time, she was appointed immediately. Her pay was $500 per year.

Ida Lewis remained at the lighthouse another thirty-two years, during which time she grew more legendary. The city presented her with a new lifeboat, and she was awarded a silver medal in 1881 for a dangerous winter rescue of two soldiers from nearby Fort Adams who had fallen through the harbor ice. The notoriety over what she considered her duty distressed her. She admitted to preferring the solitude of the lighthouse over all the fanfare. With only a dog for company in her later years, she was asked by the press why the more traditional role of wife and mother had not appealed to her. "The light is my child," she shyly replied.

In 1911, Ida suffered a stroke while tending the light and was found unconscious on the lantern floor. Hours later, the doleful sound of bells in the city signaled her death. Her funeral was attended by thousands and was, no doubt, a spectacle such as she herself would have shunned. Her bravery and service were honored again in 1924, when the name of the lighthouse was changed to Ida Lewis Rock Light; a Coast Guard buoy tender homeported in Newport, Rhode Island, also bears her name.

simple truncated octagonal cone—had proven itself at other sites in the Northeast. The tower was completed in 1797, and the President's warning about erosion has proven correct; today it stands less than fifty feet from the cliff's edge.

The number of Northeast lighthouses would increase fivefold by 1852, when the Lighthouse Board was established. This region was the foothold of America, and a rugged conical masonry design quickly became its signature. Stone and brick were strong, durable, and readily available. Wood served for lanterns and stairways early on, but was later replaced by more fire-resistant iron. Tower height varied greatly, depending on the task assigned the lighthouse and the elevation of its site. Boon Island Light, situated on a pile of rock six miles off the coast of southern Maine, rose 133 feet above the sea as the tallest in the Northeast. In contrast, diminutive Derby Wharf Light in Salem Harbor, Massachusetts, was a mere 12 feet tall. Most elevated were the Navesink Twin Lights, shining from New Jersey's Highlands at 246 feet above sea level.

Multiple light stations, introduced in 1764 at Plymouth, were used exclusively in the Northeast, where a craggy, labyrinthine coast required many beacons clustered close together. Two sets of twin towers stood in Maine, four in Massachusetts, and one in New Jersey. Triple lighthouses also stood on Nauset Beach, Cape Cod. All were established by 1838, before the United States adopted a technology to differentiate lighthouses by flashing signals. The last twins went out of service in the 1930s. Only four sets remain standing today, along with the triple lighthouses of Nauset Beach, which were restored in the 1980s and exhibited on Cape Cod National Seashore.

The nation's first wave-swept lighthouse was built in 1850 at Minots Ledge, a mile off Cohasset, Massachusetts. It was an iron pile design and a grand experiment. Never before had American engineers attempted to construct a lighthouse on a submerged reef in the open water. It stood only a year, however. An April 1851 nor'easter snapped its legs and sent it to the bottom, drowning two keepers. It was replaced by a sixty-foot wave-swept masonry lighthouse in 1860. This sentinel has survived to the present, but in its manned years was considered the worst duty for lightkeepers in the Northeast. Quarters were cramped, the tower was damp and cold, and the concussion of waves pounding its walls drove some men mad.

PLYMOUTH TWIN LIGHTS, MASSACHUSETTS, PICTURED CIRCA 1890

MINOTS LEDGE LIGHTHOUSE, UNDER CONSTRUCTION IN 1857, BOSTON

FENWICK ISLAND LIGHTHOUSE, DELAWARE

◄ ◄ (Top) The first wooden twin lights at Plymouth, Massachusetts, were built in 1769 but burned in 1801 after the oil-soaked floor caught fire. They were rebuilt, but by 1843 the walls were rotting. A third set went into service with a covered way connecting them but only the southwest twin remains today.

◄ ◄ (Bottom) America's first offshore lighthouse was completed in 1850 on perilous Minots Ledge, a submerged ledge south of Boston. The rickety skeleton tower was destroyed in a storm only a year after construction. A sturdy granite lighthouse replaced it in 1860 and survives today—the oldest wave-swept masonry lighthouse in America.

◄ Lighted in 1859, the Fenwick Island Lighthouse is the oldest existing lighthouse in Delaware.

► The candy-striped sentinel standing at the nation's most northeastern corner is West Quoddy Head Lighthouse. Known for its pea-soup fogs, the station received a fogbell in 1820.

WEST QUODDY HEAD LIGHTHOUSE, BUILT IN 1808 AND REBUILT IN 1857, ON THE BORDER BETWEEN MAINE AND NEW BRUNSWICK

Waterbound screwpile and caisson lighthouses became commonplace in Northeast bays and rivers by 1880. More than forty screwpile lighthouses were built in Chesapeake Bay alone, marking low mudflats and sandbars where rivers enter and islands intrude into shipping lanes. The little beacon at Drum Point, Maryland, was typical, a quaint octagonal house standing on iron legs in shallow water. Window boxes served as a garden for the keeper and his family; chickens and pigs were kept on a wooden platform under the lighthouse. Spring ice breakup on the bay sometimes caused problems for screwpile lighthouses like this one, as floes pushed against their metal legs. Some were even swept away and sunk.

Iron and concrete caisson foundations superceded many of the ice-vulnerable screwpile structures by 1900. Caisson lighthouses proved ideal for a number of offshore locations in the Northeast, particularly Long Island Sound and Delaware Bay. Like artificial islands, the platforms on which these lighthouses were built were solidly anchored to the bay floor to withstand battering waves and ice, and even a collision with a ship off course. The cast-iron tiered designs were nicknamed for their resemblance to familiar objects—a spark plug, telescope, or wedding cake: Orient Point Lighthouse, for example, was dubbed the "Coffee Pot" after its construction in Long Island Sound in 1899.

The apex of offshore lighthouses in the Northeast came in the 1960s with the construction of two "Texas tower" beacons—Light Station Ambrose, nine miles off New York Harbor, and Chesapeake Offshore Light Structure, fourteen miles off the mouth of the bay. Often mistaken for oil rigs, they were built on tubular legs anchored deep in the seafloor. Resident crews of Coast Guard keepers lived on these remote, modern lighthouses until the 1980s. Light Station Ambrose was rammed by a tanker in 1996 and so badly damaged it had to be rebuilt. Its successor, commissioned in 1998, is the newest sentinel in the nation.

Today, about two hundred lighthouses stand along the

THOMAS POINT LIGHTHOUSE, CHESAPEAKE BAY

Northeast Coast, beginning with candy-striped West Quoddy Head Lighthouse on Maine's northeasternmost point, and stringing southward to Fenwick Island Lighthouse a few feet north of the Mason-Dixon Line in Delaware. A variety of architectural styles and time periods are represented in these lighthouses, reflecting the diverse character of the Northeast shoreline and its long, proud maritime history.

Thomas Point Lighthouse, pictured in the late nineteenth century, was typical of more than thirty cottage-style screwpile beacons that served in the Chesapeake Bay. It remains on its original site and is the last of its kind still in service on the bay.

CHASING AWAY THE FOG

Fog silently enshrouds Portland Head Lighthouse at the entrance to Maine's busiest port. In response, the station's diaphone horn sends an ear-splitting honk seaward to guide mariners safely into the harbor.

Fog signaling was as important a task for lighthouses as keeping a bright, dependable beacon. When the air became thick and the light failed to show at its proper distance, sound became the sailor's guide. Though a benefit for ships, this meant hours of hard work and interminable noise for lighthouse families. New England and the Pacific Northwest, shrouded up to a quarter of the time, had the most fog, followed by the Great Lakes. Point Reyes Light in northern California often held the record; its horns blared more than three thousand hours some years.

All manner of contrivances were tested to penetrate the murk. Cannons were used early on, but the cost for shot was high and the sound carried poorly over water. Bells came into use in 1820 and were rung by hand, taking up much of the keeper's time and energy. Vibration from larger bells sometimes loosened paint on the walls, jiggled cups in the kitchen cupboard, and set all the metal parts of a light station humming. The drudgery was eased in the 1870s when bell-striking mechanisms came into use. The work then consisted of winding up weights in the bell tower every few hours so that the clockworks would actuate the striker.

By this time, steam-powered fog signals were in use—whistles, sirens, and horns mounted on steam boilers. The familiar two-tone nasal honk of the diaphone horn came along in the 1870s, and the multitoned diaphragm horn a decade later. For the keepers, the signals were labor intensive. Coal-fired boilers were cantankerous about starting and difficult to maintain; hours were spent shoveling coal and coddling the delicate settings. Electricity eventually eliminated the need for boilers and relieved keepers of much of the work.

Along the way, a plethora of peculiar inventions came and went. Fog trumpets served for a time at several New England lighthouses. These consisted of gargantuan wooden trumpets facing the sea. Their horrendous honks were created by bellows with a variety of energy sources to power them. At Beavertail Lighthouse in Rhode Island, the keeper's old horse plodded slowly around a windlass to pump up the air tanks. Every ten seconds, he flattened his ears in anticipation of the loud blast.

Experimental wave-actuated fog signals were installed at Whitehead Lighthouse in Maine and Southeast Farallon Light off California. The Maine signal used the rush of waves to jiggle a T-bar connected to a bell clapper. At Southeast Farallon, seawater rushing though a blowhole produced a burst of air that caused a locomotive whistle to scream. Neither device was successful, since the signals were irregular and required choppy seas to work, whereas fog usually rolled in when seas were calm.

PORTLAND HEAD LIGHTHOUSE, MAINE

The strangest invention was a Chinese pigtail hygroscope fog signal installed at Baltimore Harbor shortly after World War I. It utilized human hair as a trigger for the electrical switch of a two-thousand-pound bell. Hair responds to fluctuations in humidity by expanding and contracting, so it was reasoned that the pigtail would expand when the fog rolled in and open the switch to actuate the bell striker. Once the air dried out, the hair would shrink and close the switch. It worked, but official embarrassment over its intrusion on the dedication ceremony for the Francis Scott Key Memorial in 1921 ended its career.

Colorful comments about fog signals pepper the pages of lightkeepers' logbooks and diaries. At Point Reyes, the children used the foghorn's coal chute as a sliding board, and a mother wrote glibly that her baby's first words were not the traditional "ma-ma" or "da-da," but a roaring "be-ooohhh!" Keepers learned to pause in their conversations when the signals sounded, and often maintained the odd habit long after retirement. At Destruction Island Lighthouse, two miles off the Washington coast, a lightkeeper's bull mistook the station's new foghorn for a rival and attacked it.

No matter the sound, there was always commentary. When a new fog siren went into service at Great Captain Island in New York Harbor in 1905, letters from disgruntled shoreside residents poured in to newspapers by the hundreds. A reporter penned an opinion piece in which he likened the signal to, among other things, "the moan of a bottomless pit" and "the groan of a disabled elevator." Shipmasters entering the busy port, however, thought it "music from the angel harps of heaven."

◀ A California lighthouse keeper is pictured about 1940 inspecting his station's foghorns. The heavy concussion of the horns caused cracks in masonry and impaired hearing. One lightkeeper told of seeing a seagull knocked down as it flew by a blaring horn. All manner of contraptions were invented by the Light House Establishment to deal with fog. Boston Light had a fog cannon on station in its early years. By the mid-nineteenth century, a trumpet had replaced the cannon. Steam powered the huge bellows and produced an ear-splitting honk over the bay.

OWLS HEAD LIGHTHOUSE, BUILT 1826, ROCKLAND HARBOR, MAINE

▲ *Lightkeeper Augustus Hamor, who tended the Owls Head Lighthouse in the 1930s, had a dog that rang the station fogbell. The springer spaniel amused visitors by taking the bell rope in his teeth and giving hearty yanks. Supposedly, the dog saved a mailboat from running ashore in a blinding snowstorm by digging the clapper out of a drift and sounding the bell.*

▶ *Portland Head Lighthouse is the quintessential American sentinel. Built in 1791, it retains the pastoral look of its attended days when three lightkeepers and their families shared the spacious house. Next to the tower is the brick oilhouse, added in the 1890s to store incendiary kerosene for the lamps.*

PORTLAND HEAD LIGHTHOUSE, MAINE

◄ The 1858 Bass Harbor Head Lighthouse reposes on a picturesque outcropping of rocks at the entrance to Maine's Blue Hill Bay and Bass Harbor.

► The east tower of the Cape Elizabeth twin lights still operates south of Portland, Maine. The station gained notoriety as the subject of painter Edward Hopper. His "Light at Two Lights" appeared on a U.S. postage stamp in 1970 to commemorate the 150th anniversary of Maine statehood.

◄ Bass Harbor Head Lighthouse, Maine   ▲ Cape Elizabeth Lighthouse, Maine

CAPE NEDDICK LIGHTHOUSE, MAINE

FORT POINT LIGHTHOUSE, STOCKTON SPRINGS, MAINE

◄ ◄ *The Cape Neddick Lighthouse was automated in 1987 but remains an important icon for the nearby town of York, Maine.*

◄ *Established in 1837, the first lighthouse on Fort Point, at Stockton Springs, Maine, was a wooden tower that lasted only twenty years. It was replaced in 1857 by a square brick tower of Federal design that continues in service.*

Marshall Point Lighthouse, Maine

◄ Marking the entrance to foggy Port Clyde since 1858, the small Marshall Point Lighthouse is similar in design to other Maine lighthouses at Isle au Haut and Ram Island Ledge. In 1898 the station was the first in Maine to be modernized with a telephone.

► New Hampshire's first lighthouse was built at the entrance to the Piscataqua River in 1771. Variously called Newcastle Light, Fort Point Light, and Portsmouth Light, it served until 1804 when a wooden tower replaced it. The present forty-eight-foot cast-iron tower was constructed in 1877 and shows a fixed green beacon.

PORTSMOUTH HARBOR LIGHT, NEW HAMPSHIRE

SCITUATE LIGHTHOUSE, MASSACHUSETTS

MARBLEHEAD NECK LIGHTHOUSE, MASSACHUSETTS

◄◄ *Overlooking Cape Cod Bay, Scituate Lighthouse went into operation in 1811. During the War of 1812, the teenage daughters of the lightkeeper foiled a British attack on the lighthouse by hiding behind a sand dune and playing martial music on a fife and drum. The ruse sent the approaching soldiers fleeing and assured Rebecca and Abigail Bates a place in history.*

◄ *The 105-foot Marblehead Neck Lighthouse, built in 1895 in a busy Massachusetts fishing community, is the only skeleton tower sentinel in New England. The station dates back to 1835 when a small stone tower was erected.*

► *When first commissioned in 1797, Cape Cod's Highland Lighthouse was safely positioned 510 feet from the edge of the crumbling cliffs at Truro. By 1996, only about 30 feet separated the tower from the sea when local residents raised $1.5 million to move the 430-ton brick tower.*

HIGHLAND LIGHTHOUSE, MASSACHUSETTS

WATCH HILL LIGHTHOUSE, RHODE ISLAND

◀◀ *Though small as states go, Rhode Island has a perilous shoreline, plentiful fog, and twenty-four lighthouses. Watch Hill Lighthouse, established in 1806 and rebuilt in 1857, marks the northern entrance to Fishers Island Sound.*

◀ *Marking the point where the Narragansett Bay and Long Island Sound waters mingle, Point Judith Lighthouse guards Rhode Island's Harbor of Refuge, a place vessels sought during surprise summer storms. The tower was built in 1857 and is the fourth lighthouse to stand on the point.*

▶ *Five Mile Point Lighthouse has stood sentry over Connecticut's New Haven Harbor since 1840. Its unique spiral stairway is made of triangular granite slabs wedged in a helical pattern from the base to the iron lantern.*

POINT JUDITH LIGHTHOUSE, RHODE ISLAND

FIVE MILE POINT LIGHTHOUSE, CONNECTICUT

LYNDE POINT LIGHTHOUSE, CONNECTICUT

◄ *Completed in 1838, the Lynde Point Lighthouse marks the broad mouth of the Connecticut River. The sixty-five-foot octagonal tower has a cantilevered wooden stairway dating to 1868.*

► *The first Fire Island lighthouse, built in 1825, had an unusual eclipsing device to make it flash. The present brick tower went into service in 1858 with a first-order Fresnel lens. The exterior was coated with a layer of cement in 1871, which earned the tower the nickname "Winking Woman," for its resemblance to a lady in a long gown. The black-and-white bands were added in 1891 to distinguish Fire Island Lighthouse from its neighbor at Montauk Point.*

FIRE ISLAND LIGHTHOUSE, LONG ISLAND, NEW YORK

CAPE MAY LIGHTHOUSE, NEW JERSEY

◄ The first formal lighthouse on Cape May wasn't erected until 1822 to mark the entrance to Delaware Bay and the important channel to the port of Philadelphia. The tower lasted only fifteen years before falling into the surf. Its 147-foot successor was built safely inland and still keeps watch over New Jersey's southernmost point.

► "Old Barney" has been a popular New Jersey landmark on Long Beach Island since 1859. It was built by Lieutenant George Gordon Meade, who later distinguished himself as a Union General, defeating Robert E. Lee at Gettysburg.

BARNEGAT LIGHTHOUSE, NEW JERSEY

▼ *One of the eastern seaboard's youngest lighthouses, Harbor of Refuge Light was built in 1926 at the southeastern tip of an 8,040-foot breakwater protecting the town of Lewes, Delaware. Recently acquired by the Delaware Bay & River Lighthouse Foundation, the iron tower is being restored to the early 1960s Coast Guard era.*

► *One of "Donahoo's Dozen," comely little Concord Point Lighthouse, built in 1826, is one of seven sentinels remaining of the twelve built in the Chesapeake Bay by Revolutionary War hero John Donahoo.*

HARBOR OF REFUGE LIGHTHOUSE, DELAWARE

CONCORD POINT LIGHTHOUSE, MARYLAND

CAPE DISAPPOINTMENT LIGHTHOUSE, WASHINGTON

Lighthouses of the Pacific Coast

THE WEST COAST, ALASKA, AND HAWAII

The first lighthouse on North America's Pacific Coast was a crude beacon erected in 1837 at a Russian trading post at Sitka, Alaska. It sat atop the government house and aided the misty harbor's flourishing fishing and fur industry. Only a few years later, whalers placed a beacon at Lahaina, Maui (in what were then known as the Sandwich Islands), to assist the great fleet that plied the winter whaling grounds. It was a mere oil lantern hung from the wharf, but it gave safe entrance to the islands' most important port at the time. The raucous whalers often found it extinguished by local missionaries, who objected to their rowdy behavior. In retaliation, they fired cannonballs over Lahaina's tiny wooden church on Sunday mornings.

As feeble lights burned in the future states of Alaska and Hawaii, the West Coast between Mexico and British Columbia lay dark—but not for long. The addition of the Oregon Territory in 1848, coupled with the purchase of Upper California at the end of the Mexican War, gave the United States a 1,300-mile coastline on the Pacific Ocean. The port of Nootka, on Vancouver Island, quickly became an enclave of fortune hunters looking to profit from the Pacific Northwest's wealth of fish, fur, and lumber. Discovery of gold at Sutter's Mill in January 1848 sent a flurry of speculators and homesteaders to California. Ships laden with passengers and goods rounded treacherous Cape Horn and

headed for the West Coast, only to encounter a steep, irregular shoreline, near-continual buffeting winds, and blinding fog.

Congress responded to the rush westward by increasing appropriations for lighthouses, and ordered the construction

TRINIDAD HEAD LIGHTHOUSE, CALIFORNIA

▲ HECETA HEAD LIGHTHOUSE, OREGON

◄ ◄ *Fur trader John Meares, who was looking for the rumored "Great River of the West" in 1788, found only a fogbound shore. He named it Cape Disappointment. Four years later, the fog lifted, and explorer Robert Gray saw the mighty Columbia River. In 1856, it was marked by Cape Disappointment Lighthouse.*

◄ *Keeper Fred Harrington was photographed at the top of Trinidad Head Lighthouse during World War I. The tiny Northern California sentinel, built in 1871 at an elevation of almost 200 feet above sea, was struck by a monstrous wave in 1914 that slammed the cliff and sent seawater spewing over the lantern.*

Establishment taking place back in Washington, D.C., put construction on hold. Additional funds were secured in 1850, but work was held up again until authority was transferred to the newly created Lighthouse Board in August 1852. The Baltimore contractors Gibbons & Kelley were awarded the bid to build nine of the proposed sixteen West Coast lighthouses.

The steep, jagged coastline and deep, rough seas challenged the builders. Materials had to be landed at dangerous rocky points and hauled up cliffs. Roads were hacked out of the wilderness to connect light stations with what little civilization then existed in the West. The early lighthouses were of two basic designs—squat masonry towers and cottage-style sentinels, most standing duty on high headlands. Two exceptions to the headland location were the tip of a long sandspit jutting out from the Olympic

TILLAMOOK ROCK LIGHTHOUSE, OREGON

▲ *Nicknamed "Terrible Tilly" by its keepers, Tillamook Rock Lighthouse was built in 1880 on a stump of granite a mile off the shores of northern Oregon. Crews were put on and off the lighthouse in a breaches buoy using a derrick and boom, which also hoisted equipment and supplies. In 1957 the Coast Guard decommissioned the lighthouse. Today it is a columbarium called Eternity at Sea where the ashes of the dead are interred.*

of sentinels at the mouth of the Columbia River and in the Strait of Juan de Fuca. Additionally, Alexander D. Bache of the U.S. Coast Survey was sent to the West Coast in 1849 to locate other sites for lighthouses. He chose sixteen important points between Southern California and Puget Sound. Ten lighthouses were recommended for California, with four designated for the entrance to San Francisco alone. The remaining six were suggested for present-day Oregon and Washington, and included an important sentinel for Cape Flattery at the northwest tip of the territory.

While Bache surveyed for lighthouse sites, shipping increased and wrecks began piling up, particularly in the murky Golden Gate Strait. Merchants and ship owners implored Bache to move quickly, but a government investigation of the Light House

MILE ROCKS LIGHTHOUSE, CALIFORNIA

Peninsula at New Dungeness, and Point Pinos, situated in a little cypress grove at Monterey.

Work began on Alcatraz Lighthouse in San Francisco Bay on December 13, 1852, and the tower was completed the following year. No light shone, however, since the French glassworks were unable to keep up with the sudden demand for lenses. Complicating the issue was an error in the blueprints for Alcatraz Lighthouse and its eight bright compatriots then under construction. All had been drawn to fit the old Lewis reflector system, and their lanterns could not accommodate the larger Fresnel lenses. When the lenses finally arrived by ship, they had to be stored in San

(Continued on page 57)

POINT VICENTE, CALIFORNIA

◄ ◄ *Christened in 1906 to mark the entrance to San Francisco Bay, Mile Rocks Lighthouse was known to local residents as "The Wedding Cake." It is shown here about 1940, during an exchange of keepers from the tender (background) and a smaller launch.*

◄ *Point Vicente Lighthouse is one of the nation's younger sentinels, built in 1926 on a 125-foot bluff overlooking Los Angeles Harbor. An eerie hourglass reflection in the surrounding trees, caused by the tower's lens, gave rise to a ghost tale.*

TRAGEDY AT SCOTCH CAP

At the tip of the nine-hundred-mile-long Aleutian Islands chain lies a desolate outpost called Unimak Island, "the Roof of Hell." It's a land of active volcanoes, ice fogs, and scouring cold winds. It's also the gateway between the North Pacific Ocean and the Bering Sea, where hundreds of ships perished during the mad gold rush to Nome. Here, on a windswept, frigid point called Scotch Cap, a lighthouse was built in 1903 to help avert such disasters. It was the outermost sentinel in the nation at the time and a dreaded assignment.

At first, only two lightkeepers stood watch on the far-flung sentinel, but in 1939 the Coast Guard assigned five men to the square tower, and later built a Direction Finding Station high on the ridge behind the lighthouse. It was lonely work. The nearest village sat over a hundred miles away and the supply ship came infrequently, often delayed by bad weather. Despite the benevolent beam, shipwrecks occurred with regularity. In 1909 a fish cannery

Scotch Cap Lighthouse kept a lonely vigil at the western tip of the Aleutian Islands until April 1, 1946, when a deadly tsunami struck the station.

SCOTCH CAP LIGHTHOUSE, ALASKA

vessel ran aground in bad weather, and its crew of 194 camped around the lighthouse for two weeks before a ship came for them. A Russian freighter was stranded in 1946, its 60 survivors hosted by the Coast Guard keepers until the storm abated.

Just weeks after the freighter incident, disaster struck the lighthouse itself. In the early hours of darkness on the first of April, an earthquake rumbled beneath the island, a slight shudder that lasted only a few seconds. A weaker aftershock came a short time later. The man on watch at Scotch Cap Lighthouse dutifully recorded the events in the station logbook and notified the watchman at the Direction Finding Station on the hill. He, too, had felt the tremors. Both men thought little more about the event, since the epicenter of the quake seemed far away and no damage had occurred.

We can only speculate about what happened at the lighthouse. Perhaps Scotch Cap's watchstander went back to his reading. A cigarette burned in an ashtray on his desk, and down the hall his four comrades dozed peacefully in their bunks. Hours passed, and then a strange rustling sound was heard outside the tower, like a great waterfall cascading in the distance. The man on watch went to the door, opened it wide, and looked out into the darkness over the sea. Nothing seemed amiss, yet the hissing seemed to be growing louder and closer. And then it became a roar.

The man may have turned and headed for the radio to warn his counterpart on top of the hill. Or maybe he took several steps down the hall, intending to wake the other keepers. No one knows. Moments later a massive wave struck the lighthouse, swept up the hill, and sent seawater swirling over the floor in the Direction Finding Station. It was a tsunami, a giant wave spawned by an undersea earthquake.

The tremors the men had felt hours before had caused a huge rock shelf in the Aleutian Trench to break off in a massive undersea landslide. A column of ocean above the catastrophic event was charged with energy that could only dissipate in the form of a wave. Hardly perceptible in the open sea, the wave advanced toward the island at a speed of 500 mph. As it reached the shallows off Scotch Cap it slowed and telescoped in size. By the time it came crashing down on the point it had grown to a monstrous hundred feet high.

Electricity was knocked out at the Direction Finding Station. The crew rounded up flashlights and began checking damage. They repeatedly radioed the lighthouse, but there was no answer, nor were there any lights or signs of activity below—only darkness. Fearing the worst, they radioed the Coast Guard Station at Ketchikan: "Light extinguished and horn silent." The crew then headed for higher ground, worried that additional waves might come.

As dawn slowly illuminated the island, the fate of the five lightkeepers at Scotch Cap became apparent. All that remained of the lighthouse was a jumble of twisted wreckage. The foundation had been wiped almost clean. A thorough search was made of the station and surrounding shore, but no bodies were found. They washed up on the beach a few days later, along with much debris.

A new lighthouse was built in 1950, much higher on the point, where seismic waves cannot reach it. A memorial plaque was placed on its wall to remember the sacrifice of the five Scotch Cap lightkeepers. To avert future tragedy, a warning system was set up around the Pacific Rim (including Palmer, Alaska) to alert tsunami-prone areas when a seismic event occurs and large waves are imminent. Had it been in service on April 1, 1946, perhaps the lighthouse crew could have escaped their fate.

The lighthouse was completely destroyed and all five of its keepers died.

SCOTCH CAP LIGHTHOUSE, ALASKA

OLD POINT LOMA LIGHTHOUSE, CALIFORNIA

(Continued from page 53)

Francisco while the lanterns were rebuilt to fit them. Alcatraz Light finally went into service June 1, 1854—the first lighthouse on the West Coast. Its cottage-style design bore stark resemblance to a little Cape Cod house with a lantern rising from the roof. Finding a keeper to tend it meant offering extra money to lure candidates away from the goldfields.

Southeast Farallon Island Light, completed in 1855 some twenty-three miles off the Golden Gate, was the first offshore lighthouse on the West Coast. Here, builders were challenged by the island's steep cliffs and seabird rookeries. Angry to have their nests disturbed, the birds attacked workers as they hauled materials up a long serpentine path to the site, 355 feet above the sea. Equally angry were the egg-pickers—several companies who harvested the eggs and sold them to San Francisco bakeries. The station was a dreadful assignment for families: nothing grew in the gardens and water was scarce. (There was also the extreme isolation of the site, which proved disastrous during medical emergencies.)

At Point Loma Lighthouse in San Diego, the windy, arid terrain required construction of an eight-mile road along the four-hundred-foot cliff, so water for mortar could be brought to the dry peak. Shortly after it was placed in service, Point Loma Light was criticized by mariners who claimed that it was too elevated to be seen in fog. Ultimately it was put out of service and replaced by New Point Loma Lighthouse at the water's edge.

In 1857 the entrances to the Columbia River and the Strait of Juan de Fuca finally were marked with lighthouses. Building the latter, a sentinel on Tatoosh Island at Cape Flattery, was a formidable task. Landing was dangerous due to rocks around the island, pounding surf, and tricky currents at that confluence of waters. Local Makah refused to surrender the island, since it was where they processed whales and seals and held potlatch ceremonies. They continually bothered the survey crew. A battery was built facing the mainland, guards were posted, and the steamer *Active* periodically fired its guns over the water as a warning. Even after the lighthouse went into service in December 1857, its first four keepers resigned, citing fear of the Makah.

By 1900, fifty-three lighthouses and four lightships were standing watch along the West Coast. Monumental among them were the wave-swept sentinels built on rock pinnacles at Tillamook, Oregon, and Saint George Reef, California, which were costly to construct and dangerous to tend. Seas often breached the towers and tossed rocks onto them. Sand and seaweed clogged the foghorns. Lightkeepers and supplies had to be landed by means

(Continued on page 61)

KEEPER JAMES RANKIN

◄ ◄ *One of the original twelve West Coast lighthouses, Old Point Loma Lighthouse was lighted in 1855 on lofty Point Loma, San Diego. Mariners soon discovered it was too elevated to provide guidance in harbor fogs, but it was not abandoned until 1891 when New Point Loma Light went into service at the base of the point.*
◄ *In the late nineteenth century, the U.S. Lighthouse Board undertook a campaign to document its service. Many lighthouses and their keepers were photographed, among them James Rankin, keeper of Fort Point Lighthouse in San Francisco Bay from 1878 to 1919.*

Shedding Light on the Light

The lustrous second-order lens of Boston Lighthouse, on duty since 1859, sends a brilliant white flash seaward every ten seconds. Originally, it was illuminated by an oil lamp and revolved by means of clockworks actuated by weights suspended in the tower. Electricity has upstaged the old system. A 1000-watt bulb now provides the light source.

A lighthouse's signature is its beacon, the great light pouring from its lantern each night to guide home the weary mariner. The light may be fixed or flashing, and can incorporate a red sector to shine over a dangerous area, or be entirely red or green to mark the sides of channels. Clarity, regularity, and dependability are the watchwords. So many lights now shine over our coasts and harbors; each must be easily identifiable by a special characteristic.

Over the centuries, a variety of illuminants and lighting fixtures have been used in lighthouses. The earliest tower beacons were braziers that burned wood or coal. Candelabras containing dozens of tapers were hung in the first colonial lighthouses in the United States, followed by pan lamps and spider lamps containing reservoirs of oil with multiple wicks.

KEEPER WITH LENS (LOCATION UNKNOWN)

Dressed in a clean apron, a turn-of-the-century lightkeeper checks the lamp inside a first-order lens. The keeper's daily routine centered on the beacon, which had to be cleaned and refueled each morning, then monitored throughout the night.

Lightkeepers had to keep the many wicks trimmed so that they burned clean and clear and, thus, earned the nickname "wickies."

Individual oil lamps followed, placed in front of silvered reflectors to enhance their light. Circular wicks helped channel air for a more efficient flame. Later, small lenses were positioned in front of the lamps and reflectors to further magnify the light. Whale and fish oil were the most popular fuels, but lard oil, colza seed oil, and rapeseed oil (made from rapeseed or turnip seed) were also used.

BOSTON HARBOR LENS

Until the 1820s, all lights were white and fixed, since there was no technology to make them flash, and they seldom could be seen for more than a few miles. This changed when French physicist Augustin-Jean Fresnel developed a revolutionary lenticular system. He used mirrors and prisms to bend and focus light into bright rays. His magnificent beehive-shaped catadioptric apparatus surrounded a single oil lamp and could transform its feeble light into a piercing beam visible as far as thirty miles out at sea.

Fresnel constructed lenses in six sizes, called orders. A first-order lens (the largest size) served a seacoast light, while a sixth-order lens was suitable for a small harbor beacon. Later, titanic hyper-radiant lenses were developed for important landfall lights, such as Hawaii's bright beacon at Makapu'u Point. Fixed lenses had a smooth barrel of magnifying glass for a continuous beam, while flashing lenses were composed of a series of magnifying bull's-eyes that broke the light into individual beams that appeared to flash as the lens revolved. If timed properly, they gave the lighthouse a unique signal.

Fresnel lenses were heavy and turned on bearings or chariot wheels. Larger models floated in tubs of mercury, which is low in friction and high in density. A clockwork system with weights suspended in the tower, similar to a cuckoo-clock mechanism, kept the lens revolving at a specified rate. The keepers wound up the weights every few hours, and as they fell the lens turned. During the day when the light was off, there was considerable work to do, cleaning the prisms and brass and maintaining the gears of the clockworks.

Oil lamps as light sources were replaced by incandescent oil vapor lamps in the 1880s and acetylene gas lamps in the 1890s. Electricity began to appear early in the twentieth century, but many of the old prism lenses still continued in service utilizing electric lightbulbs. Automation, beginning in the 1950s, brought

CAPE MEARES, OREGON

smaller, more durable plastic lenses that worked on the same principle as the classic Fresnels. They required little care, however, and could be exposed to the weather.

Myriad sensors and timers were devised to turn the electric lights on and off as needed, and rotate replacement lightbulbs into position when old ones burned out. Solar panels also replaced external power sources at many remote lighthouses. Such progress has rendered all active lighthouses self-sufficient and made the job of the lightkeeper obsolete. Coast Guard Aids to Navigation Teams visit lighthouses every few months to check the automatic equipment; otherwise, the lights run on their own.

ARANSAS PASS, TEXAS

KILAUEA POINT LIGHTHOUSE, HAWAII

(Continued from page 57)

of a derrick and boom, and after several fatal accidents at these dangerous lights the Coast Guard automated them.

Acquisition of the Alaska and Hawaii territories launched a frenzy of new construction, as the Lighthouse Board hurriedly marked these far-flung shores. Molokai Light was built next to Hawaii's leper colony, and became symbolic of hope for the sick and abandoned. The "Tombstone Twins" of Alaska's Unimak Island, as lightkeepers woefully dubbed the sentinels at Scotch Cap and Cape Sarichef, were the loneliest lighthouses in the nation and the most difficult places to serve; manned only by men, they were visited but once a year by a supply ship.

Among the last lighthouses to be built in the Pacific was the steel-skeleton tower light at Cape Kumukahi on Hawaii's Big Island, constructed in 1934. Though an otherwise pleasant assignment, a grave danger lurked nearby. In 1960 an eruption of Kilauea sent lava over the cape and destroyed the keeper's house. The tower, remarkably, was spared when local Hawaiians gave offerings to the volcano's red-haired goddess, Pele, and the flow forked around the lighthouse. Thereafter, the sentinel was known as the Lucky Lighthouse.

Today, the five states of the West are home to 103 lighthouses. Though neither as numerous nor as old as their cousins on the East Coast and in the Great Lakes, they are monuments to westward expansion and the pioneering spirit of America. A third of them stand in California, where the world's busiest port, Los Angeles, handles millions of tons of cargo each year. Almost as busy are the Strait of Juan de Fuca and Puget Sound, the deep gateway to Seattle where thirteen lighthouses shine. Tallest of the Pacific lighthouses is 148-foot Pigeon Point Light at Pescadero, California, while the brightest is Hawaii's Makapu'u Light on Oahu, where the nation's only hyper-radiant lens sends a beam almost forty miles over the sea. Hawaii also lays claim to the tiniest sentinel in the nation, Ka'uiki Light at Hana, Maui. Its Hawaiian name means "the glimmer."

◄ *The "Big Eye of Kauai" is the Kilauea Point Lighthouse, built in 1913 on the island's northernmost point.*

▼ *Built in 1881 as a coastal beacon to mark the Kaiwi Channel between Molokai and Oahu, Laau Point Light was an isolated station in its early years. The original stone tower was rebuilt twice. This nineteen-foot pyramidal wood tower served after the light was automated in the 1930s. Today, the Laau Light shines from an uninteresting fiberglass pole and is solar powered.*

LAAU POINT LIGHTHOUSE, HAWAII

TRINIDAD HEAD MEMORIAL LIGHT, CALIFORNIA

▲ *Trinidad Head Lighthouse, north of Eureka, California, was so beloved by local residents they built a memorial replica of it in 1948 along Coastal Highway 1.*
► *When an elder lighthouse on a high bluff at Point Loma was unable to pierce the fog that sometimes plagues San Diego Harbor, New Point Loma Lighthouse was built in 1891 at a lower elevation.*

New Point Loma Lighthouse, California

◄ Pigeon Point Lighthouse, California

▲ Umpqua River Lighthouse, Oregon

Named for the beautiful clipper ship Carrier Pigeon, *wrecked here in 1853, Pigeon Point Lighthouse is one of the tallest sentinels on the West Coast, towering a stately 115 feet over a rock-riddled shore near Pescadero, California.*

Beautiful Umpqua River Lighthouse rises above the trees in an Oregon park that bears its name. Built in 1894, it replaced an earlier tower that fell victim to erosion. The sixty-five-foot lighthouse holds a magnificent two-ton first-order Fresnel lens manufactured in Paris. Its light is visible twenty miles at sea.

CAPE MEARES LIGHTHOUSE, OREGON

▲ Handholds built into the window frames of Cape Meares Lighthouse at Tillamook Bay, Oregon, attest to the hazards faced by old-time lightkeepers as they cleaned windows. In the 1820s, the Light House Establishment authorized handholds for the most dangerous stations. The useful grips were commonplace by 1890 when Cape Meares received its lighthouse.

► YAQUINA HEAD LIGHTHOUSE, OREGON

One of the most visited lighthouses in the nation is Yaquina Head Lighthouse at the mouth of the Yaquina River, Oregon. In 1931, lightkeeper John Zenor reported 14,196 visitors at the station. In recent years, even greater numbers have turned out for the tower's periodic public openings. A dramatic seascape and a noisy lighthouse ghost, whose footsteps are often heard on the stairs, are among the attractions.

▼ *A mere mile off the Oregon Coast, Tillamook Rock Lighthouse seems a cozy ocean retreat, but only the toughest men endured its isolation and heavy weather. It was one of the first lights in the nation to be decommissioned.*

▶ *To amply mark the treacherous Columbia River entrance, North Head Lighthouse went into service in 1898, joining with its older sister sentry at Cape Disappointment only a few miles away. The Spanish-style tower was designed by Carl W. Leick, who designed and built twenty-four lighthouses in the Pacific Northwest.*

TILLAMOOK ROCK LIGHTHOUSE, OREGON

NORTH HEAD LIGHTHOUSE, WASHINGTON

CAPE HENRY LIGHTHOUSES, VIRGINIA

Lighthouses of the South

VIRGINIA TO TEXAS

Low, flat beaches, rolling dunes, and vast marshes are the hallmarks of the southern coastline. With few physical landmarks to guide them, but plenty of dangers lurking just offshore, early settlers knew lighthouses were essential for safe passage. A string of shoals along the Outer Banks of North Carolina quickly earned the unflattering nickname "Graveyard of the Atlantic." The Florida Reef, a shallow bed of coral stretching from Key Biscayne to Key West, was equally daunting. Numerous river estuaries—including the Cape Fear, the Savannah, the St. Johns, the Sabine, and the mighty Mississippi—were impeded by shallows and sandbars and, in summer, cyclones wheeled up the coast or into the Gulf of Mexico. Complicating navigation was the Gulf Stream, which hugged the coastline from Key West to Cape Hatteras, causing southbound ships to sail close to shore to avoid its five-knot northward push.

The first lighthouses in the South were built before the American Revolution, at Charleston Harbor, South Carolina, in 1767 and Tybee Island, Georgia, in 1771. They were among the tallest sentinels of their day, for no lofty headlands exist in the South to provide elevation for a tower. Heat, mosquitoes, and lack of good freshwater thwarted their builders and plagued the lightkeepers. Indians often were hostile, and hurricanes were an annual threat; additionally, building materials had to be brought from the Northeast by ship, with no beacons to guide them to a new site. But southern pioneers were desperate to export the riches of their land and bring in needed goods. A legion of southern sentinels grew, slowly but steadily.

Lighthouses were established before 1803 at several important spots—Cape Henry and Hampton Roads on the southern Virginia shores of the Chesapeake Bay, Cape Hatteras and Ocracoke on the Outer Banks, and Bald Head at the entrance to the Cape Fear

▲ MATAGORDA ISLAND LIGHTHOUSE, TEXAS

CHANDELEUR ISLAND LIGHTHOUSE, LOUISIANA

◄◄ The lighthouses at Cape Henry, Virginia, are reminders of the Lighthouse Establishment's long dedication to mariners. The elder sentinel, built in 1791, was the first public works project undertaken by the first Congress of the United States. When an earthquake sent cracks up its walls, the time-worn old tower was abandoned and a second, taller lighthouse was built nearby.

◄ The approach to the Mississippi River passes was marked by Chandeleur Island Lighthouse in 1855. In 1891, a hurricane wheeled over the island, and the keeper was trapped for three days but kept the beacon lit. Following the storm, the lighthouse was torn down and replaced by a more wind-resistant skeleton tower.

► The soft, alluvial soil of the Gulf Coast demanded special foundations for lighthouses. A heavy masonry tower built at Sabine Pass on the Louisiana side of the Sabine River in 1857 was fortified with flying buttresses to distribute its weight.

SABINE PASS LIGHTHOUSE, LOUISIANA

resulted in a flurry of lighthouse construction. By 1825, five lights had gone into service between St. Augustine and Key West, plus one at Pensacola. Increased traffic into the Mississippi River, coupled with Texas statehood in 1845, further expanded the bastion of beams in the South. Alabama got its first lighthouse at Mobile in 1822, and two more at Choctaw Point and Sand Island a decade later. Cat Island off Mississippi received its first sentinel

CARL SVENDSEN, KEEPER OF ST. SIMONS LIGHTHOUSE FROM 1907 TO 1935

River. A fledgling effort to mark the mouth of the Mississippi River began in 1810 with a small light at Bayou St. John leading into Lake Pontchartrain. It was the first lighthouse in the Louisiana Territory, but not being visible at the river entrance, it failed to reduce shipwrecks. Eight years later, a coastal beacon was placed at Franks Island, Louisiana, near Northeast Pass. It was the most expensive lighthouse built to that date by the U.S. government, at $85,000, but its builders soon learned that the soft soil would not support the heavy masonry. It was replaced years later by a screwpile lighthouse.

By 1820, fourteen lighthouses stood in the South, a commendable number yet less than a fifth of the nation's lighthouses. The addition of the Florida Territory in 1821

in 1831, as did Pass Christian just east of Bay Saint Louis. By the time Texas's first lighthouse flashed on at Sabine Pass in 1856, thirty-two lighthouses were shining in the Gulf of Mexico and Mississippi River Delta, and a third of the nation's sentinels stood in the South.

Many had risen at great risk. In Florida, the Seminole Wars took a toll on life and property, as did storms. The brick sentinel on Key Biscayne was attacked and burned by a Seminole raiding party in 1836; one keeper was killed and the other badly burned. A decade later at Sand Key, nine miles off Key West, a hurricane leveled the lighthouse and killed its keeper, his daughter and grandson, and two visitors. Realizing masonry was unsuitable for the fickle key, the Light House Establishment tried a new pile design for the replacement tower.

Pile-and-caisson technology was gaining acceptance at this time in the rivers, sounds, and backwaters of the South where small, cottage-style sentinels stood on wooden straight piles or metal screwpiles. Along "Hurricane Alley," where Sand Key reposed in the hot sun, the solution was a larger screwpile design firmly anchored into the coral reef. Six such "Iron Giants" would be built on the Florida Reef between 1852 and 1879, the tallest standing at 142 feet. Their keepers lived in small box-shaped houses set within the splay of iron legs. Freshwater was caught on the roof of the cupola and stored in a cistern; food was mostly fish and sea turtles. Heat, sunburn, and loneliness beset the men, and their only link with shore in the age before radio was the carrier pigeon.

As foundries in the North turned out more and more iron in the mid-nineteenth century, it became the preferred material for lighthouse construction nationwide, but especially in the South, where rapid shoreline changes necessitated relocation of lighthouses. A collapsible iron design served well for sites like Hunting Island, South Carolina, and Cape Canaveral, Florida. These towers were fabricated in pieces, shipped to their sites, and quickly and cheaply assembled. When the shoreline changed, they were disassembled and moved to new sites to better serve shipping. The mettle of such towers—their strength and durability—was proven beyond a doubt by the tall iron

SABINE BANK LIGHTHOUSE, TEXAS

◄ *Fondly called "The Texas Spurkplug," the Sabine Bank Lighthouse marked the shoals seventeen miles off the entrance of the Sabine River. Manufactured in Detroit and shipped in pieces, the lighthouse went into operation in 1906. Its lantern was removed in 2002.*

▼ *As early as 1820, busy inland riverbanks and backwaters were marked with small post lights, and keepers called lamplighters were hired to tend them. Minnie Meissner had been tending this Mississippi River post light near Pevely, Missouri, for twenty-five years when the Coast Guard photographed her in 1940 for a press release.*

LAMPLIGHTER MINNIE MEISSNER

73

► Though its keeper's dwelling is boarded up and ramshackle, Cape San Blas Lighthouse is still operational as a beacon for Florida's St. Joseph Bay.

► ► Old Key West was a raucous town in the early 1800s, home to a large fleet of wreckers and fishermen, as well as pirates and mooncussers, who preyed on passing ships. When Florida became a territory in 1821, Key West was among the first sites selected for a lighthouse. Lighted in 1825 on Whitehead Point, the old sentinel survived countless storms and political changes until an 1846 hurricane leveled it. A sixty-foot brick tower replaced it two years later (shown about 1880). An additional twenty-six feet of height was added in the 1890s.

CAPE SAN BLAS LIGHTHOUSE, FLORIDA

the lighthouse by day, was created by coating aluminum siding with a durable porcelain material. Its 28-million candlepower beacon is the most powerful in the United States.

Like great cathedrals of light, southern sentinels are tall and proud. Ninety-two remain standing, stretching from Jones Point Light at Alexandria, Virginia, to Brazos Santiago Light on the Texas–Mexico border. Fifteen are more than 150 feet high. The best known is lofty Cape Hatteras Lighthouse, soaring 200 feet over Cape Hatteras National Seashore. It is visited by thousands of vacationers each year and beloved for its handsome black-and-white spiral daymark, a dress that helps distinguish it from the many other sentinels on this stretch of coast where lighthouses are separated by a mere ten to twelve miles. "Lady Hatteras," as southerners call her, made news in 2000 when, for a hefty price tag, the 2,800-ton tower was moved back from the water's edge to prevent its collapse into the sea.

▼ The first sentinel built in South Carolina marked the entrance to Charleston Harbor in 1767. It stood almost a century before storms and Civil War cannon fire ruined it. A stately brick tower replaced it in 1876. Morris Island Light Station was a pastoral assignment in the 1880s when this photo was taken, but the island has since washed away, leaving the tower standing in water and in danger of collapse.

KEY WEST LIGHTHOUSE, FLORIDA

sentinel at Bolivar Point, Texas. During the great Galveston Hurricane of 1915, it sheltered sixty-five people on its stairs, and was the only structure still standing on Galveston Island when the storm ended.

The nation's newest onshore lighthouses were built in the South. The cylindrical reinforced concrete lighthouse at Oak Island, North Carolina, was constructed in 1958 to provide safe passage into Wilmington. Piles were driven 125 feet into bedrock to anchor it, and a dual-intensity beacon ranging from 1.4 million to 14 million candlepower was installed in the lantern. Sullivans Island Lighthouse at Charleston, South Carolina, was built in 1964 to replace the aging Morris Island Light. Given a unique triangular shape, it is the first and only lighthouse in the nation with an elevator. The black-and-white daymark, a paint scheme to identify

MORRIS ISLAND LIGHTHOUSE, SOUTH CAROLINA

HAUNTED LIGHTHOUSES

Hardly a lighthouse stands that does not have some lurid tale of restless spirits prowling its dark interior. The ambience of a lonely tower begets such legends—shadows lurk and echoes resound in the night, damp recesses emit fetid odors, wind squeals through cracks in the windows and walls, and all manner of tragedies fill the pages of its logbook.

St. Simons Lighthouse in Georgia is renowned for the phantom footsteps on its stairs, popularly attributed to a lightkeeper murdered at the station in 1880. A rocking chair is said to rock by itself at Battery Point Lighthouse in California; and a lovely specter believed to be the spirit of a young girl who vanished inside Oregon's Yaquina Bay Lighthouse in the 1890s now dances in the garden on moonlit nights.

Farther up the Oregon coast at Heceta Head Light, the infamous wrinkled visage of the Gray Lady is seen at the attic windows of the keeper's house from time to time. Ethereal Civil War soldiers sit on the porch of Point Lookout Lighthouse in Maryland, only a short distance from a graveyard where prisoners of war were buried. At Fairport Harbor Lighthouse on Lake Erie, a smoky ghost kitten skitters about the second floor of the quarters, chasing a ball of crumpled paper tossed out by museum staff.

Among the most terrifying (yet comical) lighthouse ghosts was Captain Johnson, the poltergeist at lonely, waterbound Carysfort Reef Lighthouse. The 112-foot screwpile sentinel went into service in March 1852 on a shallow coral reef at the eastern end of the Florida Keys. It was the first of several "iron giants" built in the South to mark offshore hazards along notorious Hurricane Alley. The first keeper, Charles Johnson, was a retired sea captain and, according to those who knew him, "a great sinner." He died at the lighthouse only a short time after his appointment.

The assistant keeper took over and was soon joined by a greenhorn assistant. The new man had been on the lighthouse only a few nights when a terrifying uproar began. It had been an exceptionally hot day, and the two keepers were grateful when night came and the temperature began to drop. The head keeper volunteered to take the first watch and sent the assistant to bed. But shortly after dark, a horrid screech and long, low moan coursed the tower, jolting the assistant awake.

He rushed to the watchroom and asked the head keeper if he, also, had heard the horrible noise. The head keeper admitted

THE STAIRWAY OF OLD PRESQUE ISLE LIGHTHOUSE, MICHIGAN

that he had, but seemed unruffled by the clamor. He calmly told the novice keeper about the untimely death of Captain Johnson a few weeks earlier, plus the details of his wayward life. The sounds heard in the tower were, according to the head keeper, cries of contrition from the restless spirit of old Captain Johnson.

Almost nightly, the torment continued for the remainder of the summer. It seemed to abate in the autumn and was seldom heard in the winter months. But when hot weather returned the next year, the ghost of Captain Johnson again went on the rampage. His ghost was never seen, only heard. But what a roaring voice the wretched old man had as he wailed sorrowfully on hot summer nights!

So it continued for nearly a century—the ghost relatively subdued in winter and on the rampage in summer. Keepers learned to live with the tower's harmless resident poltergeist and passed down his legend year after year to new men assigned to the remote lighthouse.

In 1927, a visitor named Charles Brookfield spent the night on the tower and heard the infamous ghost. He was told the story of Captain Johnson, but not being a believer in the supernatural, he rejected the tale and set out to find the real cause of the noise. After a few hours of listening to the unsettling sounds and examining the tower from top to bottom, he had a theory.

"Under the hot sun, the tower's iron walls expand; in the cool of darkness, they contract," said Brookfield. He reasoned that the quick shrinking of the metal as it cooled down after dark caused joints to rub and created sounds that were "startlingly human."

Captain Johnson, it seemed, was merely a product of a structural response to rapid temperature change. His ranting was most severe in summer, when temperature extremes were the greatest. The explanation made sense, but lightkeepers scoffed and continued to tell the ghost tale. Fiction, in this case, was much more fun to believe than the truth.

◄ ◄ *Lighthouses are prime real estate for ghosts. One of the most frequent haunts is the spiral stairway, where phantom footsteps and strange echoes are heard, where shadows play and musty odors linger. The rough-hewn granite stairway of Michigan's Old Presque Isle Lighthouse harbors a glowing specter said to be the spirit of a former caretaker.*

◄ *The iron screwpile lighthouse at Carysfort Reef, Florida, was home to Captain Johnson, the restless spirit of the tower's first keeper, who died only a few weeks after his appointment to the waterbound tower in 1852. Crews endured his horrid moans and snarls until the lighthouse was automated in 1960.*

ASSATEAGUE ISLAND LIGHTHOUSE, VIRGINIA

◄ *The bright barber pole daymark of Assateague Island Lighthouse helps it stand out against the verdant tide marsh of Virginia's eastern shore. Originally established in 1833, it was rebuilt in 1867. The tower has a unique lift system alcoved into its walls that allowed lightkeepers to hoist heavy oilcans from the base to the lantern.*

► *The last lighthouse built in North Carolina went into service at Whalehead in 1875. The Currituck Beach Lighthouse is similar in design to its tall sister sentries farther south on the Outer Banks. The 163-foot sentinel was among the nation's first lighthouses to be automated. Minus resident keepers, it quickly fell prey to vandals and the elements. Acquired by the Outer Banks Conservancy in 1981, it has been lovingly restored and opened to the public.*

CURRITUCK BEACH LIGHTHOUSE, NORTH CAROLINA

CAPE HATTERAS LIGHTHOUSE, NORTH CAROLINA

◄ *The tallest sentinel in America, Cape Hatteras Lighthouse has marked the Outer Banks, known to seamen as the "Graveyard of the Atlantic," since 1870. It stands 198 feet tall with 268 cast-iron steps leading to the lantern. In 1999, the massive tower was moved to a safe site 1600 feet back from the sea to prevent the encroaching waves from undermining it. The $12 million project required a year of planning but a mere twenty-three days for the actual move. The tower was ceremoniously relighted in November 1999 and reopened to the public six months later.*

► *Rumored to be named for the many bodies that have washed ashore during shipwrecks, Bodie Island received its first lighthouse at Oregon Inlet in 1848. Poorly built, it had to be replaced a decade later. The second tower stood only two years before Confederate troops dynamited it. The present 156-foot lighthouse was built in 1872. Now part of Cape Hatteras National Seashore, it is open to visitors. A museum in the keeper's house details the site's history.*

BODIE ISLAND LIGHTHOUSE, NORTH CAROLINA

OCRACOKE LIGHTHOUSE, NORTH CAROLINA

◄ Ocracoke Island has a colorful past, beginning with Native tribes who created monstrous shell mounds and wild horses that swam ashore from shipwrecks in the 1600s. The notorious pirate Blackbeard used the island as a retreat and was captured here in 1718 and executed. A lighthouse was approved for Ocracoke in 1789 with the convening of the nation's first Congress, but the tower was not built until 1803. Called Shell Castle Island Light, it was destroyed by lightning in 1818. The current Ocracoke Lighthouse, built in 1823, is the oldest active sentinel in North Carolina.

► Known for its unique diamond daymark, Cape Lookout Lighthouse was built on Core Banks in 1859 to guide shipping into Beaufort. Its predecessor, built in 1812, wore an equally colorful daymark of red and white horizontal stripes. The lighthouse is part of Cape Lookout National Seashore and houses a small museum in the keeper's quarters.

Cape Lookout Lighthouse, North Carolina

CAPE FLORIDA LIGHTHOUSE, FLORIDA

◄ *Cape Florida Lighthouse on Key Biscayne is the oldest structure in South Florida and the oldest operating lighthouse in the state. Built it 1825, its pioneer history is scarred by tragedy. In 1836, angry Seminoles set fire to the tower and killed one of its two keepers. The other was marooned on top of the lighthouse after its wooden stairs burned. He was rescued by a passing ship three days later, and though badly burned, survived. The lighthouse is part of the Bill Baggs State Recreational Area.*

► *Export of cotton through Florida's Apalachicola Bay spurred construction of a lighthouse on St. George Island in 1834. It was the first of three light towers that would battle hurricane winds and moving sand. The light's inadequacy forced the government to build a taller tower at Cape St. George in 1848, but three years later it was undermined in a storm. The third and present tower was constructed from the ruins of its predecessor in 1852. Over the years, its foundation weakened and caused it to lean. Demolition plans were in the works in the late 1990s when the Cape St. George Lighthouse Society raised money to straighten the tower.*

CAPE ST. GEORGE LIGHTHOUSE, FLORIDA

ST. MARKS LIGHTHOUSE, FLORIDA

ST. AUGUSTINE LIGHTHOUSE, FLORIDA

◄ ◄ St. Marks Lighthouse watches over Florida's Apalachee Bay and the entrance to the St. Marks River. Built in 1842, it was only a year old when a hurricane destroyed the dwelling and sent keeper J. P. Mungerford and his family into the tower for safety. After the storm, the house was rebuilt and the entire station was enclosed by a protective seawall. The lighthouse continues to operate and is open to the public as part of St. Marks National Wildlife Refuge.

◄ A sentinel for America's first city and the oldest lighthouse site in Florida, St. Augustine Lighthouse was established in 1824 on the ruins of a seventeenth-century Spanish watchtower. Rebuilt in 1871, the 167-foot sentinel attracted migrating birds, which sometimes collided with the lantern and broke windows. A more frightening event occurred in 1886 when the tower was rocked by an earthquake that stopped the lens from revolving. Restored as a museum in 1993 by the Junior Service League of St. Augustine, the lighthouse is a popular tourist stop.

PENSACOLA LIGHTHOUSE, FLORIDA

◄ *Pensacola Harbor was the site of one of the earliest colonies on the Gulf of Mexico, but a lighthouse wasn't built here until 1824. Its first keeper was Jeremiah Ingraham, whose wife, Michaela, took over in 1840 and served fifteen years. A new lighthouse was built in 1858 at a cost of $45,988, a princely sum at the time. It survives today, surrounded by the Pensacola Naval Air Station.*

► *Biloxi has been a tourist town for most of its life. Wealthy vacationers from New Orleans and Mobile came to its shores by boat in the early 1800s, their pilots guided by a huge magnolia tree. A Congressional bill sponsored by Mississippi representative Jefferson Davis resulted in the manufacture of a cast-iron lighthouse that was shipped from Baltimore and assembled in front of the aging magnolia tree in 1848 to serve coastal traffic. A survivor of countless storms, the Civil War, and road construction, it stands in the center median of Highway 90.*

BILOXI LIGHTHOUSE, MISSISSIPPI

SHIP ISLAND LIGHTHOUSE, MISSISSIPPI

◄ *The wooden lighthouse at Ship Island off Mississippi was built in 1886 to replace a crumbling brick tower that had gone into service in 1853. Though wood traditionally deteriorates quickly in salt air, the tower's sturdy beam and brace construction lasted until 1972 when it caught fire. The present tower is an exact replica of the 1886 lighthouse, built by the Friends of the Gulf Island National Seashore.*

► *The Tchefuncte River pours into Lake Pontchartrain near Madisonville, Louisiana, a once-busy stop for steam ferries plying the lake. The first lighthouse here was inaugurated in 1838 and lasted until Civil War gunfire damaged it beyond repair. A new Tchefuncte River Lighthouse went into service in 1868 with a spacious dwelling, fogbell tower, and oilhouse. Only the lighthouse remains standing.*

Tchefuncte River Lighthouse, Louisiana

NEW CANAL LIGHTHOUSE, LOUISIANA

◄ *Louisiana's New Canal Lighthouse marks the manmade waterway connecting Lake Pontchartrain with New Orleans. A beacon was established here in 1839 just as the canal opened, and was rebuilt in 1855 and again in 1890. For much of its career, the lighthouse was tended by capable feminine hands. Caroline Riddle is remembered for her courage in the terrible 1915 hurricane, and Maggie Norvell was commended for bravely rescuing survivors of a tour boat fire in 1926.*

► *A shadow of its former self, Sabine Pass Lighthouse has fallen into decay since its decommissioning in 1952. Lighthouse preservationists worry that this old guardian, unique for its flying buttress design, will be lost. The tower once shone a light over the Louisiana border at the Sabine River. If saved, it will celebrate its 150th birthday in 2007.*

SABINE PASS LIGHTHOUSE, LOUISIANA

BOLIVAR POINT LIGHTHOUSE, TEXAS

◄ *Texas's busy port of Galveston received an iron sentinel in 1852 on Bolivar Point, but the light was too feeble and too short. In 1858, its height was raised to 177 feet and a third-order Fresnel lens was installed. Confederates dismantled the entire lighthouse three years later and melted down the metal. A new tower went up in 1872. It is renowned for its benevolent service during the great hurricanes of 1900 and 1915. In the latter storm, sixty-five people took refuge on the lighthouse stairs after their homes were destroyed.*

► *The Aransas Pass Lighthouse, leading into Corpus Christi, was completed in 1855 after great debate as to its location and design. Damaged in the Civil War, repair operations suffered a setback in 1867 when a Texas Blue Norther—an intense cold snap—struck the area. Hundreds of birds took refuge in the tower. A shift in the channel rendered the lighthouse obsolete in 1952. It was sold to a private owner and has been renovated and relit.*

ARANSAS PASS LIGHTHOUSE, TEXAS

MATAGORDA ISLAND LIGHTHOUSE, TEXAS

◄ Six lights were established in Matagorda Bay over the years, the most prominent at Matagorda Island, south of the bay entrance. Its black cast-iron tower was first illuminated in December 1852, then given a colorful daymark of red, white, and black bands in 1854. The lighthouse began to lean a decade later and was dismantled and moved to its present site in 1873. Insects, attracted to the beacon, were a persistent problem at the station. In 1918 a keeper wrote of removing dead bugs from the lantern "by the shovelful."

► Halfmoon Reef Lighthouse once marked a shoal separating Matagorda and Palacios Bays. Built in 1858, it was lit sporadically until 1942 when the Coast Guard discontinued it permanently and a local historical group had it moved ashore at Port Lavaca. The exterior was restored as an Eagle Scout project.

HALFMOON REEF LIGHTHOUSE, TEXAS

OLD PRESQUE ISLE LIGHTHOUSE, MICHIGAN

Lighthouses of the Inland Seas

THE GREAT LAKES AND LAKE CHAMPLAIN

"Inland Seas" aptly describes the Great Lakes and Lake Champlain, for they possess much of the character of small oceans. Deep water, a dangerous coast, storms, and fog are found there, sometimes equal to or worse than that along saltwater coasts. For this reason, a third of the nation's lighthouses stand on lakeshores. Michigan alone has 112 lighthouses, the most of any state in the nation.

The rivers connecting the lakes to inland areas became crucial portals for trade and settlement soon after the American Revolution, but it wasn't until about 1820 that Lake Champlain opened to navigation and the Midwest began to grow rapidly. People came by trail and river routes to settle along the lakeshores of Vermont and New York, or homestead on the flatlands of Ohio and Indiana. The first lighthouse to guide them was a crude tower attached to a building at Fort Niagara in 1818 to mark the point where the Niagara River flows into Lake Ontario. A year later a stone tower was built at Presque Isle, Pennsylvania, on a finger of land enclosing a natural bay in Lake Erie. To meet the demand of increased travel, another lighthouse was built at the entrance to the Grand River on Lake Erie in 1825. This was the gateway to the Western Reserve, a fertile tract of land in Ohio.

That same year, the Erie Canal opened, linking Buffalo to the Hudson River and New York City. Emigration stepped up, aided by steamboats. Travel between Lake Erie, Lake Huron, and Lake Michigan was relatively easy, since all three are at about the same level. The St. Clair and Detroit Rivers provided a navigable connection between Lake Erie and Lake Huron, and Lake Michigan

▲ LENS IN OLD PRESQUE ISLE LIGHTHOUSE

RACINE REEF LIGHTHOUSE, WISCONSIN

◄ ◄ *Built on Lake Huron in 1840 at a bargain price of $5000, Michigan's Presque Isle Lighthouse marked a harbor by the same name and served until 1871, when a taller tower upstaged it. It's now a museum with resident caretakers.*

◄ ▲ *A bull's-eye in the lens of Old Presque Isle Lighthouse is dark, having given over its duties to a newer lighthouse in 1871. The rugged old sentinel strangely reactivated itself in 1979, forcing the Coast Guard to disconnect power to the defunct beacon. Local boaters attribute the unexplained event to a ghost that haunts the tower.*

◄ *In the days before mechanized icebreaking, shipping on the Great Lakes closed every winter and did not resume until the spring thaw. The Light House Establishment rushed to remove lightkeepers from their stations before ice set in. An 1880s photo of Wisconsin's Racine Reef Lighthouse shows the station's three keepers pushing a boat full of supplies over the ice to shore. The big freeze came early that year, preventing the tender from docking. The crew and their wives walked ashore.*

POINT IROQUOIS LIGHTHOUSE, MICHIGAN

was then easily accessed via the Straits of Mackinac. By 1829 when the Welland Canal and its series of locks opened to allow access to Lake Ontario (some 330 feet higher than Lake Erie), fifteen lighthouses stood on the two lakes. The Soo Locks at Sault Sainte Marie opened navigation into Lake Superior in 1855, and increased ship traffic hastened the completion of the lake's first lighthouse at Iroquois Point that same year.

More than four million tons of cargo per year moved over the Great Lakes at this time, and seventy-six lighthouses were on duty. The opening of canals and locks encouraged settlement and resulted in enormous growth in commerce. Lumber, ore, and grain came east while hordes of emigrants went west, all on ships aided by the region's lighthouses. By 1860, one-third of the nation's population lived in the five states surrounding the Great Lakes and about a fifth of all U.S. lighthouses stood there.

Lake Champlain saw a similar rise in water transportation, linked to trade in furs, lumber, and stone. Vessels accessed the lake from the north via the St. Lawrence and Richelieu Rivers, and from the south via the Champlain Canal, which was built to connect the lake to the Hudson River. Its first lighthouse went into service on Juniper Island near the burgeoning port of Burlington in 1826, followed by a beacon on Isle La Motte three years later. By 1871, when Colchester Reef Lighthouse was built on a stone caisson a mile out in the lake from Shelburne, twelve lighthouses were shining over its waters.

Most of the inland lighthouses were built of stone or brick, for these materials are abundant in the region. The great breadth of the lakes and the harsh conditions vessels experienced there, particularly in winter, demanded sturdy, reliable beacons that could withstand powerful winds, grinding ice, and punishing extremes in temperature. Lightkeepers had to be of stalwart constitution, too. Prior to the mid-twentieth century (when icebreaking became a regular winter activity on the lakes), keepers worked only part of the year, since the shipping season ended the first of December and did not resume until the first of

◄ *Point Iroquois Lighthouse began service in 1857, guiding shipping into the St. Marys River and Soo Locks of Lake Superior. The station was so isolated in its early years, the government opened a small school for the keepers' many children. The light was discontinued in 1962 and turned over to the Hiawatha National Forest, which operates it as a museum.*

▼ *Standing vigil over the confluence of Lake Huron and Lake Michigan, Old Mackinac Point Lighthouse showed a beacon from 1892 until 1957, when lights on the newly built Mackinac Bridge rendered the old sentinel obsolete. Now part of Lakeshore Park, its old fog-signal building has been turned into a gift shop filled with lighthouse trinkets to delight summer tourists.*

OLD MACKINAC POINT LIGHTHOUSE, MICHIGAN

BIG SABLE POINT LIGHTHOUSE, MICHIGAN

April or later. Winter storms and ice conditions made water travel too dangerous. Lighthouse keepers were removed from their posts as soon as possible after shipping shut down in December.

On many occasions, winter arrived with a fury before the first of December. Ice cloaked the towers and sealed them shut, entombing their human attendants until a tender crew arrived and removed the ice. Such scenarios played out seasonally at pierhead and offshore lighthouses where the full force of lake winds and waves buffeted. Stannard Rock Light in Lake Superior and Spectacle Reef Light in Lake Huron were the most dangerous assignments. Both were built on stone caissons miles from shore, and were the first lighthouses to be evacuated for the winter due to their remoteness and the difficulty of docking. In 1913, Stannard Rock Light was frozen in by the end of November. The tender *Amaranth* had to anchor more than half a mile away and send a crew in a pulling boat to the edge of the ice jam, from which they hiked some distance to the lighthouse and chipped away with pickaxes for several hours before freeing the lightkeepers.

Lightkeepers of offshore lights sometimes stayed at their posts for part or all of the winter to reduce the cost of renting quarters ashore, even though there was no work to do. Walter Button, keeper of Colchester Reef Light, was unable to get ashore for a doctor for his wife in January 1888 when his youngest child was born. A few winters later, his successor, a bachelor named August Lorenz, had his evening reading interrupted by a spar of ice that pierced the wall of the lighthouse like the bowsprit of a ship, then retracted into the darkness. It tore his rowboat from the davit and tossed it onto a cake of ice. Lorenz spent most of the following morning chasing the ice cake with a long pole in hand, trying to snag the boat. His persistence was rewarded.

Today, 226 lighthouses stand in and around the Great Lakes and 10 on Lake Champlain. Those still in commission are automated and remain on duty throughout the year, periodically checked by the Coast Guard, whose heavy-duty icebreakers keep the shipping lanes open even in the worst freeze conditions.

◄ *A major beacon for shipping headed south on Lake Michigan to Chicago, Big Sable Point Lighthouse has served since 1867. Part of Ludington State Park, it is a popular destination with beachcombers, who willingly trek almost four miles round-trip in loose sand to climb the tower's 130 steps. Their reward is a bird's-eye view of the lake.*

▼ *Perched at the tip of a long concrete pier, South Haven South Pier Lighthouse marks the south side of the entrance to the Black River on Lake Michigan. The little red tower was built on shore in 1903 and moved to the end of the pier in 1913.*

South Haven South Pier Lighthouse, Michigan

LUDINGTON NORTH PIERHEAD LIGHTHOUSE, MICHIGAN

Though Lake Champlain's importance to shipping has not kept pace with that of the Great Lakes, it remains a viable route to the Atlantic via the Saint Lawrence Seaway. Sentinels on the Great Lakes are critical to navigation, for more than 250 million tons of freight travel the lakes annually, most of it iron ore. The Soo Locks alone handle more tonnage each year than the Panama and Suez Canals combined! Huge supercarriers wend their way through the maze of canals and locks connecting the lakes to bring valuable cargoes to major ports for shipment to all parts of the world. Even in an age of high-tech navigation, with every imaginable modern instrument at their fingertips, crews of these huge vessels still look to lighthouses for reassurance.

FORT GRATIOT LIGHTHOUSE, MICHIGAN

◄◄ *In winter, Ludington North Pierhead Lighthouse becomes an ice castle, as wind and waves cover it in a glistening frozen mantle. The white steel 1924 tower sits on a black concrete caisson and marks Ludington Harbor. It replaced an earlier lighthouse, built in 1871.*

◄ *A marker for the mouth of the St. Clair River where it meets Lake Huron, Fort Gratiot Lighthouse was erected in 1829 after the first lighthouse on this site collapsed. The tower was improved and heightened in 1861 and continues in service as part of a larger Coast Guard complex.*

LIGHTSHIPS

Before engineers could build lighthouses on offshore sites, lightships were anchored over perilous spots in the sea-lanes. A combination of lighthouse and ship, lightkeeper and sailor, this unusual fleet served American waters for nearly a century and a half.

The first lightships to serve in U.S. waters were anchored at Willoughby Spit, Virginia, and Northeast Pass, Louisiana, in 1820. They were small boats with a single mast to which a lantern was attached. A lamplighter rowed to them nightly to kindle the beacons and returned at dawn to extinguish them. Later, revenue cutters were refitted as lightships, and permanent crews were enlisted.

By the 1860s, two sizes of lightships were in use. Small vessels displaced a hundred tons or less; larger lightships were as big as three hundred tons. "Inside" lightships served in rivers, bays, and sounds; larger "outside" lightships were anchored off the coastline miles at sea. The first such outside lightship in the nation was assigned in 1823 to the busy sea-lanes off Sandy Hook, New Jersey, on the approach to New York Harbor.

Lightships were named for the stations where they anchored—*Hen and Chickens, New South Shoals, Umatilla, Barnegat, San Francisco, Frying Pan Shoals,* to name a few. Numbers identified them as well, especially where a station had more than one lightship on duty. Relief lightships were towed from station to station, and did substitute duty when the regular vessel was sent into port for maintenance or repair.

The trademark of the lightship was its light basket or light cage. Most vessels had two, mounted near the tops of masts. Early beacons used gimbaled oil lamps that remained level as the ship rolled. These were filled on deck and then hoisted up the masts on their own little pulley systems. Later, gas and electric lights with small lenses increased brilliance.

The vessels possessed little or no motive power, since lightships were designed to remain in one spot. Bulky, flattened hulls with bilge keels reduced rolling in heavy seas, and huge mushroom-shaped anchors held the vessels on position, digging firmly into the seabed. Heavy storms or moving ice sometimes dragged the anchor, or parted its chain, setting a lightship adrift. In 1913, a Lake Erie lightship vanished in a storm and was later found on the bottom of the lake, its crew lost. A similar fate befell the *Cuttyhunk* lightship off Cape Cod in 1944.

Less tragic was the storm-tossed journey of the *Columbia River #50.* It broke anchor in a storm and went aground on Cape Disappointment in November 1899. The Lighthouse Board gave it up for lost, but a house-moving company in Portland, Oregon,

LIGHTSHIP *HURON*

hoisted it onto a specially made railway and moved it a mile overland to Baker Bay, where it was refloated and placed back in service. The company received $17,000 for the effort.

Lightships also were vulnerable to collisions with ships, for they worked in busy shipping lanes. *Ambrose* lightship on the approach to busy New York Harbor was hit most often, but the damage usually was minor. More serious tragedies occurred at Long Island Sound's Cornfield Point, where a lightship was sunk in 1919, and the Nantucket Shoals, where the liner *Olympic* struck the #117 in 1934 and sent it to the bottom.

Lightship duty was monotonous and dangerous. Crews of six to twelve men, nicknamed "fish," lived on board in crowded quarters and worked long hours without any change in scenery, even during the worst weather. During bouts of fog, bells and horns deprived the men of sleep. Seasickness plagued some, since lightships rolled constantly. And like all seamen, they missed their families during the long weeks of duty at sea.

The dangers of duty on lightships, and their expense, encouraged the development of other technologies to mark offshore perils. Screwpile-and-caisson lighthouses, large buoys, and Texas towers eventually replaced lightships. One by one

LIGHTSHIP *OVERFALLS*

they were decommissioned, until the last surrendered its duties to a large navigation buoy on Nantucket Shoals in 1987.

Those that remain have easier assignments now, as museum pieces at places like the Baltimore Maritime Museum, South Street Seaport in New York, and Columbia River Maritime Museum in Astoria, Oregon. The old *Overfalls* lightship that once served off Delaware is now the headquarters of the U.S. Lighthouse Society in San Francisco. This unique breed of ship may be gone from the sea, but it's definitely not forgotten.

LIGHTSHIP *SAN FRANCISCO* #70

◄ *Painted with the name Overfalls, in memory of a vessel that once served off the Delaware Bay, a lightship provides nautical interest to a waterfront park in Lewes, Delaware. Lightships moved from station to station as navigational needs changed, and took on new names. This vessel did duty in Connecticut and Massachusetts waters before being acquired by the city of Lewes.*

◄ *Shackled to the seafloor by a large mushroom-shaped anchor, the lightship San Francisco #70 was stationed off the Golden Gate in 1898. Its double lights, held in cages at the top of the masts, helped distinguish it from nearby Farallone Lighthouse's single white light.*

SPLIT ROCK LIGHTHOUSE, MINNESOTA

◄ Built in 1910 to serve ore freighters headed into Duluth, Minnesota, Split Rock Lighthouse sits 130 feet above Lake Superior on a rocky promontory. High concentrations of magnetite in the rocks along this section of the lake played havoc with ships' compasses, necessitating construction of the lighthouse.

► The Grand Marais Front Range Lighthouse and its rear companion (not shown) are leading lights for ships making entry into West Bay from Lake Superior. The thirty-four-foot steel front light was the first of the two to be built in 1895 and served as a single harbor light until 1897 when the rear light was added, creating a range.

GRAND MARAIS FRONT RANGE LIGHTHOUSE, MINNESOTA

SAND ISLAND LIGHTHOUSE

Sand Island Lighthouse, situated at the western end of the Apostle Islands of Lake Superior, was a lonely outpost in 1882 when its first keeper moved into the brownstone house with attached tower. Weather here could be punishing. In December 1919, the lighthouse tender Marigold rescued the lighthouse family after a series of late autumn storms prevented the vessel from docking at the station to remove its crew for the season. Nearly all their food was gone, and coal to heat the house had been used up.

Sand Island Lighthouse

WIND POINT LIGHTHOUSE, WISCONSIN

◄ *Ships approaching Racine Harbor, Wisconsin, from the north were unable to see a dangerous point of land jutting into Lake Michigan until Wind Point Lighthouse was built in 1880. The beacon has a white flashing coastal light, but also a red light to warn of Racine Reef. Its keeper's house now serves as the town hall for the small hamlet of Wind Point.*

► *Michigan's Port Sanilac Lighthouse on Lake Huron is an octagonal fifty-nine-foot brick tower attached to a brick house. This coastal light was built in 1886 and has a fourth-order Fresnel lens manufactured in Paris by the firm of Barbier & Fenestre. Though the light still operates, the site is privately owned.*

PORT SANILAC LIGHTHOUSE, MICHIGAN

EAGLE HARBOR LIGHTHOUSE, MICHIGAN

◄ Eagle Harbor Lighthouse was constructed on Michigan's Keweenaw Peninsula in 1871 for a mere $4000. The small tower did not last and a new lighthouse went into service in 1871. With the addition of a fog signal in 1895, two assistant keepers were hired. They were forced to rent quarters in town, since the house would only accommodate the family of the principle keeper. The tower has a white daymark on its lake side and can be accessed from both floors of the house.

► Au Sable Point juts into Lake Superior in Michigan's Upper Peninsula. Put into service in 1874, Au Sable Point Lighthouse was automated in 1958 and its lens removed. The optic was returned to the tower in 1996 at the behest of local citizens. The lighthouse is located in Pictured Rocks National Lakeshore.

AU SABLE POINT LIGHTHOUSE, MICHIGAN

115

STURGEON POINT LIGHTHOUSE, MICHIGAN

◄ *Sturgeon Point extends into Lake Huron a few miles north of Harrisville, Michigan. Its lighthouse has stood watch over the shoal formed by the point since 1869. Rising seventy feet, it is connected to a small keeper's house by a covered passageway. Families served here until 1939 when the Coast Guard automated the beacon. The Alcona Historical Society now owns the property and operates a small museum in the keeper's quarters.*

► *Lake Michigan's eastern shore is marked by Little Sable Point Lighthouse, near Silver Lake. The beautiful 1874 brick tower, standing 107 feet tall, is all that remains of a once-large complex. In 1955, the Coast Guard automated the station and razed its ancillary buildings to discourage vandalism.*

LITTLE SABLE POINT LIGHTHOUSE, MICHIGAN

MANISTEE NORTH PIERHEAD LIGHTHOUSE, MICHIGAN

◄ Lake Manistee is connected to Lake Michigan by the Manistee River. Marking its mouth is Manistee North Pierhead Lighthouse. It's a small tower—only thirty-nine feet tall—with a big name. In its attended years, the cast-iron sentinel was accessed from shore by a 300-yard-long iron catwalk elevated above the concrete pier to protect keepers from the large waves that sometimes pummel the jetty. Even so, it was a long walk carrying heavy cans of oil on a cold, windy night.

► Considered one of Lake Michigan's loveliest lighthouses, Point Betsie Lighthouse guides ships in and out of Manitou Passage. Built in 1858, the site is often blustery. Its comfortable dwelling was home to families until 1983 when automation was completed. It was the last manned lighthouse in Michigan.

POINT BETSIE LIGHTHOUSE, MICHIGAN

POINTE AUX BARQUES LIGHTHOUSE, MICHIGAN

◄ *A guidepost to Saginaw Bay, the 1857 Pointe Aux Barques Lighthouse sits on a rocky point overlooking Lake Huron. The name, given by French traders, means "point of little ships." After 1876, lightkeepers here worked in tandem with the crew of a nearby lifesaving station. Their services were desperately needed in 1913 when the* Howard M. Hanna, *with thirty-three people aboard, went aground off the lighthouse. All were safely rescued.*

► *A waxing crescent moon sets over Lake Huron behind the seventy foot Tawas Point Lighthouse. Often called Ottawa Point Light, the tower was illuminated in 1876 to mark Tawas Bay. It replaced an earlier lighthouse that was rendered useless by shifting sands. The beacon is a fourth-order Fresnel lens made in France in 1880. Once driven by clockworks, it is now powered by an electric motor.*

TAWAS POINT LIGHTHOUSE

◄ Marquette Harbor on Lake Superior became a boom port in the 1850s when rich deposits of iron ore were discovered in the nearby hills, and the St. Marys Falls Ship Canal opened at Sault Sainte Marie. Three lighthouses were built to mark the harbor. The main beacon is Marquette Harbor Light, built in 1866. Its spacious house was enlarged in 1906. Keepers of this lighthouse also tended the lower harbor breakwater light south of the station.

► The oldest continuously operating lighthouse on the Great Lakes stands on Marblehead Peninsula, Ohio, marking the entrance to Sandusky Bay. The Lake Erie sentinel was commissioned in 1821 to help vessels safely pass a series of islands that extend north from Marblehead and to provide succor to sailors caught in the intense storms that often assail this part of the lake.

MARQUETTE HARBOR LIGHTHOUSE, MICHIGAN

MARBLEHEAD LIGHTHOUSE, OHIO

ERIE LAND LIGHTHOUSE, PENNSYLVANIA

◄ *Pennsylvania's piece of lakeshore is small, but dangerous. Three lighthouses have guided ships into the port of Erie, the oldest one established on the south shore of the harbor in 1819. Called Presque Isle Lighthouse, the name was later changed to Erie Land Lighthouse. It was rebuilt in 1857 and again a decade later. In 1899 it was discontinued permanently and later had its lantern removed. The city has created a park around the defunct tower and fabricated a replica lantern for it.*

► *Guiding traffic into Presque Isle Bay at Erie, Pennsylvania, since 1927 is the tapering square tower of Erie Pierhead Lighthouse. It has operated automatically since its inception, one of few lighthouses in the nation never tended regularly by a resident keeper. A black band distinguishes it from nearby Presque Isle Lighthouse, a white square tower.*

►► *The limestone tower standing guard over Buffalo Harbor on Lake Erie is the oldest building in Buffalo in its original location and is featured on the city seal. Built in 1833, it was joined by a breakwater light in 1872. During Prohibition, government agents used the lighthouse as a lookout for rumrunners.*

ERIE PIERHEAD LIGHTHOUSE, PENNSYLVANIA

BUFFALO MAIN LIGHTHOUSE, NEW YORK

▶ *As sunset falls over Delaware Breakwater East Lighthouse, no light comes to life in the tower's lantern. Like many aging sentinels that have outlived their usefulness, its guidance is no longer needed. The beacon was discontinued in 1996 after 111 years of faithful service, warning of shallows in the inner harbor.*

Delaware Breakwater East Lighthouse